He said,
She said

GIGI
GORGEOUS

HARMONY BOOKS
NEW YORK

He said, She said

LESSONS, STORIES, AND MISTAKES FROM MY TRANSGENDER JOURNEY

Published in the United States by Harmony Books, an
imprint of the Crown Publishing Group, a division of
Penguin Random House LLC, New York.
crownpublishing.com

Harmony Books is a registered trademark, and the Circle
colophon is a trademark of Penguin Random House LLC.

Library of Congress Cataloging-in-Publication Data
Names: Lazzarato, Gigi, author.
Title: He said, she said / Gigi Lazzarato.
Description: New York : Harmony, [2019]
Identifiers: LCCN 2018015482 (print) | LCCN
    2018031450 (ebook) | ISBN 9780525573432 (ebook) |
    ISBN 9780525573425 (trade pbk.)
Subjects: LCSH: Lifestyles. | Human behavior. | Wit and
    humor.
Classification: LCC HQ2042 (ebook) | LCC HQ2042
    .L395 2019 (print) | DDC 302—dc23
LC record available at https://lccn.loc.gov/2018015482

ISBN 978-0-525-57342-5
Ebook ISBN 978-0-525-57343-2

Printed in China

Book and cover design by Sonia Persad
Cover photograph by Warwick Saint
Photographs on the following pages by Warwick Saint:
17, 18, 19, 37, 38, 39, 57, 58, 73, 74, 75, 87, 94, 95, 101, 102,
115, 116, 117, 133, 134, 135, 149, 150, 173, 174–175, 187, 188,
202–203, 204–205
All other photographs are courtesy of the author

10 9 8 7 6 5 4 3 2 1

First Edition

To my mom, Judy.

I wish you were here,
but I know you're watching.

I love you.

I have to say, I'm really super-excited for you to read my book. It's totally balls-to-the-wall, out-to-lunch, unabashedly *me.* Completely unfiltered Gigi. Just the way we all like it (well, most of us).

But I'm also a little worried you're going to read the next couple hundred pages or so and think, this bitch just *did it*. She set out a plan for her life of what she wanted to happen in it—you know, success, celebrity, romance, love—and just *figured it out*. It's what a lot of transgender girls hope to achieve with their lives. Hell, it's what a lot of people hope to achieve with their lives. And let's get one thing straight: I'm not being cocky. I'm actually the most humble person I know. But even writing some parts of this book I've had to step back and be like "Whoa, I did that? That's crazy!" It still seems like a fairy tale to me.

The truth is: It may have looked easy, and sometimes I may *make* it look easy, but it hasn't always been like that, and I still face challenges every single day. I've had my own speedbumps. I've had my own problems. I've had to come out of the closet multiple different times for multiple things. First, for being gay. Then for being transgender. Then for being a lesbian. That's a lot of opening and closing the closet door. My arms are starting to get tired, honestly. But at least they look great, don't you think?

I'VE HAD MY OWN PROBLEMS.

What's more, my mom died way too young, and she never got to know the real me. And that makes me sadder than I can convey with words. That I never got to look in her eyes and say, "Mom, I am a transgender woman." That she never got to meet the Gigi I became.

That's who I'd like to give to you with this book. The real Gigi. But I want you to know that I don't take any blessings that I've been given in my life for granted. I thank God every day for making me as busy and stressed and fulfilled as I am. And I thank you for taking the time to read what I've written. I hope you enjoy it. Now let's get into it.

GIGI-isms

Before we jump into this gossip sesh that the publishing industry has decided to call a book, there are some things you should know about the way I communicate. First of all, you should know that a lot of people think I speak my own language.

It's a version of English, yes. But there are a lot of words I use that you don't really hear other people using. Or, typically, when they use these words, they use them differently than I do. I'd say they use them wrong and I use them right. Or correctly, if we are using proper grammar. But you shouldn't count on me for proper grammar, either.

One other thing you should know about is my extremely extensive vocabulary, which I've had to develop because of constantly having to describe beauty products on my YouTube channel. When I do talk about products, I'm usually talking about things that I *like*. If I were anybody else anywhere and my name were not Gigi Gorgeous, I would probably also totally overuse the word *gorgeous*. But I can't do that, because it would be a little too on the nose. Not that I have my original nose. But we'll get to that later, too.

When I'm speaking, I want my feelings to be conveyed and completely understood. It's also a lot about intonation, as in *how you say* whatever it is you're trying to say. Anyway, here are some of the words that are in heavy flow rotation at the moment. (Do you see what I did there? Heavy flow?)

Let's call them Gigi-isms. Practice them. Use them in your everyday conversation. Call your girlfriends and test them out! The point is, in just a few short moments, you, too, can be *speaking Gigi*!

If I were anybody else anywhere and my name were not Gigi Gorgeous, I would probably also totally overuse the word *gorgeous.*

EVERYTHING I honestly don't know when I started using this word. It just happened. Barbara Kopple noticed it when I was filming my documentary. That's how the title *This Is Everything* happened. It's self-explanatory. It means things are coming together. The situation is perfect. It's singlehandedly the best description I can give to anything. Like "The weather recently has been so nice. It's everything" or "My outfit to the VMAs was everything."

Get it? Good. We can move on, then.

DOPE/SICK/TURNT These are all kind of the same thing. They all describe when something's amazing. For instance: "This 134 MAC makeup brush is turnt. I love the way it did my contour" or "That's sick."

OBSESSED When I'm into something, I'm often "obsessed." Here's an easy one: "Nicole Richie is carrying a Balenciaga Weekender? I'm obsessed with her. And that bag."

TOTES I like to use this as a short form of *totally*. It's faster to say and sounds cuter. "Oh, you can't go out tonight? That totes sucks" is much more efficient than "Oh, you can't go out tonight? That totally sucks." See how much time I saved there? It's genius.

LIVING/DYING Despite what they mean in real life, these words are surprisingly interchangeable. I can say "I'm living for this Taco Bell Crunchwrap Supreme" or "I'm dying for this Taco Bell Crunchwrap Supreme," and, in my not so humble opinion, I'm basically saying the same thing. I will also occasionally do a variation and say something to the effect of: "Oh my God, this Taco Bell is so life right now. I was so hungry and it tastes so good. I'm dead."

Now we're getting kind of advanced. I hope you have enough brain cells to last you the rest of this list. I sense some are being killed off.

EEK-A-DEEK I say this when there's awkward tension in the room or a bad situation is going on. Or when something comes up that I don't want to have anything to do with. For instance, I'm in a room with two friends and they're fighting. I'd say, "Eek-a-deek, this is super totes uncomfortable." Yes, you can use two Gigi-isms in one sentence.

FUCKED This is also a term that is easily interchangeable. If something is bad, it's "fucked." As in, "When she said that your hair looked greasy, that was really fucked." But "fucked" can be something that's really good, too. Like "Oh my God, your Guiseppe Zanotti six-inch heels are fucked."

A GAG Something dramatic or unbelievable. "It's such a gag that my dad came with me to get my boobs. I couldn't believe it." Or more simply and generally put: "Oh my god, that was such a gag."

HUUUP! I recently invented this term because it's the sound that came out of my mouth when I was trying to hold in a laugh at an inappropriate time. For example, if someone asks you if you ate the last cupcake in the box, and you did, you would simply respond "HUUUP!" You're clearly guilty, but you're trying to divert attention and you hope the other person laughs and doesn't get mad. You can also use this in an awkward situation. Like, say a friend is confronting her boyfriend about cheating on her. Randomly, mid-conversation, you could say "HUUUP!" and run out of the room. Then you're free to not be bothered by that situation anymore.

A MOMENT Something you need to set aside time in your brain for. Something that's really going to be a memory. "This fashion brand invited us to Coachella and we're going for the first time ever. It's going to be a moment" or "We should all wear white on the Fourth of July and make it a moment."

W-W-W-WAIT Pretty self-explanatory. "W-w-w-wait. That bag from the Row costs fifty thousand dollars? You've got to be kidding me." I visualize this one to be like a car going one hundred miles an hour and then suddenly slamming on the brakes and skidding to a halt, but, like, verbally.

HUNDO P Short for a hundred percent. Used for emphatic effect at the end of a sentence or a particularly confident phrase. "I want to go to Poppy tonight and party. Hundo P." I will probably use it many times in this book, just because I'm totes into it right now and it's used for things that are certain, like the facts about my life in this book.

VIBES My friend August and I use this a lot. It's what we want to evoke. What we're shooting for. We usually use it when it comes to style and creating a look. "We're going to the AMAs and I really want Nicki Minaj/ Kim Kardashian vibes" or "The holiday party we're planning needs to give Winter Wonderland vibes."

A) I CAN'T AND B) I WON'T Absolutely no freaking way is this happening. Another way of saying flat-out "no." Like "Someone said that we should take the subway to the party. A) I can't and b) I won't."

OUT TO LUNCH This is a term I've started using within the past year or so. It's usually used when I'm talking about someone being crazy or doing something I don't agree with. "Girl, did you see her last night? She was out to lunch."

COO-COO-CA-CHOO When someone or something is completely crazy. Not just out to lunch but out to dinner and after-dinner drinks. For example, if you're out with a new friend and she starts complaining about how annoying the media is when, in fact, the only article ever written about her was one she posted about herself on Instagram, she's *hundo P* coo-coo-ca-choo.

GET INTO IT A term I use a lot before I show someone something and I want them to like it as much as I do. Like "Oh my God you need to watch this music video, but get into it, though." It can be used to cheer someone up, too, like "You totes don't need your ex-boyfriend. Let's go out. Get into it."

EXTRA It's about being dramatic and over-the-top. "I'm going to wear extensions to the floor and put on three sets of lashes tonight because I want to be extra." Be forewarned: We will come back to the concept of "being extra" several times throughout the course of this book.

1

LET'S JUST DIVE
IN ALREADY

xoxo
Gigi

Gigi wears an I.Am.Gia bikini, Make Up For Ever HD Foundation Stick, Tarte Tartelette In Bloom Eyeshadows, Anastasia Dipbrow, Lilly Lashes Miami, Givenchy Noir Couture 4 in 1 Mascara, MAC Myth Lipstick, MAC Under the Sheets Lipglass

One of the earliest memories I have of how I knew I was "different" was when I was two or three years old. My given name was Gregory. Gregory Allan Lazzarato. And I asked my two brothers Adam (older) and Cory (younger) to call me Kim. Okay, maybe I was four. But I made them swear to me that they would call me only Kim.

"Guys, my name is Kim," I would tell them. "And you'll only address me as Kim."

They obeyed me. I have absolutely no idea why I chose that name. It was completely random. This was before there was such a famous Kim in the world. Kim Kardashian, who, as you may or may not know, is my favorite Kardashian.

I had other tics, too. I would take washcloths and put them around my head with an elastic band and pretend I had long hair like the Disney princesses I admired so much. Now that I get to use hair extensions all the time, it sounds crazy that washcloths could give me the feeling of long flowing princess hair, but back then it did the trick.

One morning, when I was six, I painted my fingernails with my mom's nail polish. I just wanted to have beautiful nails and I loved the process of daintily brushing the polish and holding out my fingers to let them dry. But once my nails had dried, I realized people would see them. Instinctively, I knew that that would not be okay. Eventually, I went downstairs with my nails curled in so that no one could see—or so I thought. My brothers were eating breakfast and couldn't care less what I was up to, but my mom knew something was going on.

She handed me the phone to talk to my grandmother and I took it with my fingers still curled in. My mom grabbed the phone back from me and asked, "Are you trying to hide your nails?" And then she yelled at me because it was her nail polish that I'd used. "You have to take that off before you go to school!" I ran back upstairs crying because I didn't know how to get the nail polish off. I scrubbed my fingers with soap for what felt like hours. I was traumatized. I was embarrassed. And she never apologized.

Adam, myself, and my mom.

I don't think she looked at it as a gender thing. I'm sure the word *transgender* was not in her vocabulary. And I don't think I saw it that way, either. It was just self-expression. I wanted to look and feel pretty. She didn't think it was a serious issue, which is probably pretty typical. Parents don't understand this kind of stuff unless they are super-totes-enlightened.

My older brother, Adam, says that our mom knew I was gay from a really early age. Or, at least, she always knew I was different from my brothers. She'd buy me Barbie dolls and Spice Girls stuff without question. She knew I loved the Little Mermaid. Typically, straight boys aren't into those kinds of things. So my mom supported my interests without getting that it wasn't just about sexuality, it was about gender.

We went to Disney World as a family when I was really young. I remember it was so hot out. We were walking around to see all the different characters and take pictures with them. I was so fixated on the Little Mermaid. Out of all us kids, I was the only one who wanted to meet Ariel. I finally made my brothers and parents join me in the humongous line to meet her. We were in that line forever and my mom told everyone, "We're just going to do this, even if it's hot and boring. This is what your brother really wants to do." She knew how important it was to me, even if maybe it's not the most normal thing in the world to have a son who's obsessed with the Little Mermaid. And when I finally got a chance to meet the real Ariel that day, I was just beaming and so happy.

When I was about to turn eight, my parents asked me where I wanted to have my birthday party. I wanted a gymnastics party. I don't know where I even learned that having a gymnastics party was an option, but gymnasts are girly and gorgeous. Of course I was attracted to that.

My mom set up the gymnastics party. No one said that a boy shouldn't have a gymnastics party. My brothers didn't say that, my mom didn't say that, my dad didn't say that. We just had it.

I had absolutely no shame in my game about my gymnastics party, but when I got to the party, it was all girls. It was just me and girls. The boys in my class didn't show up. I hadn't expected this at all. So at that party, I realized I was attracted to something that mostly girls were attracted to, and I felt uncomfortable about it. Maybe there was just a little shame, too. But I don't remember anyone acting as if I should be embarrassed or ashamed. And from my perspective now, that means my family did a very good job taking care of me. And that's a lesson I apply to my friendships and relationships today. I might not understand everything that's going on with someone I love, but there's a way to be supportive even when you haven't a clue.

Me being absolutely fabulous at the water park with Adam.

Anyway, at the gymnastics party, an instructor suggested I should try diving. She mentioned it to my mom, at least, who brought it up with me. Gymnastics in the water? That felt so Little Mermaid. I said "Hell, yes!" Or whatever an eight-year-old says when he's excited about something.

The next week we went to visit a diving class. I instantly fell in love with it. It was the best of both worlds. Gymnastics in the water. I loved the smell and the sounds. I loved the buzzer that goes off. The platforms layering on top of one another. It was all so exciting. Not everyone in the class was super-flexible when it came to the actual diving, but what they did was so graceful and beautiful anyway. And everyone was also just really nice.

My mom organizing my fourth birthday party.

But, sure, I knew somewhere in my head that this wasn't a sport that boys typically took part in. That first day, I feel like I saw only two guys in a pool out of forty girls. I didn't say anything. Why should I? I wanted to learn how to dive.

I had two coaches. Misha was a Russian man with a mustache and a thick accent no one could understand. The other was a younger, hipper, more muscular, and more attractive coach with swagger. He taught the people who were less advanced. His name was Arturo. He was the one who worked with me when I was younger.

It was Arturo who made me feel bad about my gender and sexuality.

At this point I was about nine, and all of the other divers were girls. Arturo would often make me feel like I wasn't *man* enough, that I was a sissy and needed to change. Whatever that means, anyway. He was the first adult, the first person in a position of power, who made me think that way. And on this one day, at a diving competition in Vancouver, I was standing around doing something with my hair. Fiddling with it, trying different styles.

And Arturo came up to me and said, "You're one of the few boys on this team. You have to behave like a man." I was taken aback. I was a little bit stung, though I put it aside. I didn't think hard about what he'd said. It's not like my self-esteem was shattered—I got plenty of positive attention for being myself—but it made me realize, it confirmed for me yet again, that I was different. That I wasn't necessarily behaving like my assigned gender all the time. That behaving like a man wasn't my natural state. That I had to *work* at behaving like a man.

I guess he also knew something about me that he didn't know I knew. That maybe I didn't necessarily *feel* like a man, or even a boy, either.

After a few years of working with Arturo, Misha became my coach. As I said, it's mostly a female-dominated sport, but there were always a handful of young male divers around. We were all really good.

One of them—let's call him Hank—was my first real crush. We didn't go to school together. We weren't on the same team but we went to a lot of the same meets. I practiced diving outside of my regular school day, since it wasn't a sport sanctioned by the actual school. As far as I know, to this day Hank is straight out of his mind. I don't mean that he's crazy. Although maybe he is crazy. I just mean: Hank likes girls, and supposedly he liked them then, too.

Just from being around each other every once and a while, Hank and I learned that we had a lot in common. So much in common. We found the same things funny. Sometimes we would stay up until four in the morning laughing on Instant Messenger. And we would always get in trouble when we were staying at hotels for competitions because he was so loud and I would make him laugh late at night.

There was a travel meet when I was probably thirteen or fourteen; Hank was seventeen. My dad stayed at a hotel, but Hank and I stayed in a family's home—a mom, a dad, and two young kids. I don't know why that happened—it's just how it worked out. It was cheaper to stay with a family than to stay in a hotel. The family was there at the house where we stayed. It was weird. So weird.

We got to the house around dinnertime. I remember it was dark out, and I started crying to the parents that I was homesick. I didn't understand why

I had to stay there when my dad was at a hotel. "I hate this," I said. "This is awful." I must have seemed so rude, but really I was just young and didn't know how to express myself. The family must have calmed me down enough that I was functional and showed us to our room. There were single beds for each of us. And when we went to bed that night, Hank put on porn. I was shocked.

We'd shared rooms before. But that was the first time he'd ever put porn on the TV. We'd talked about what girls we thought were "hot" and stuff, but we had never, *ever* watched porn. And that's when he asked me, "Do you want to jerk off?"

Frightened and intimidated, I just said yes.

I was trying to act really into it. Like I had totes done it before. So we started "jerking off." It was so dark in the room and we were both under the sheets of our beds so I couldn't see him, but from the sounds of it, he was getting *really* into it. "Yo, are you about to cum?" he asked me. I wasn't turned on at all and had never cum before. But I just went along with it.

"For sure," I said.

He started moaning really loudly, and I heard the bed squeak. Before I knew it, he had cum.

I knew it was time for me to cum, too, so I gave it a few beats and then started mimicking his moaning and fake-came.

"I just came everywhere," I announced.

In the moment I had no idea what I was doing, so I guess I took it upon myself to make it the most convincing first ejaculation I could have. I did what I could: I literally peed on myself. He got up to get a towel and clean himself off and then stuck his arm out to pass me the same towel. Grossed out (like, ew, who does that!) but not showing it, I grabbed the towel from him and cleaned the pee from my stomach and quickly threw the towel on the floor next to my bed.

That night passed. After that, if there was a diving thing we both had to be at, sometimes Hank and I would end up staying in a hotel room together. We'd be in for the night. We would get ready for bed, and when it was time to go to sleep, he would always find a random porn channel.

"Oh, yeah, it's porn time," Hank would say.

I think that first night was the all-clear for him. Since I hadn't said anything the first time we'd masturbated together, he thought it was like "our thing" or something. So when the lights went down, we'd jack off.

Nova Scotia, New York, those kinds of places.

We'd usually stack extra pillows between us to block our view of each other. And at this point, I wasn't faking it anymore. I was fully functional, fully masturbating, and fully into it. And one night when we were doing it at the same time, I looked over at him.

"Why are you looking?" he asked. I wasn't sure if he was mad or joking. But then he made eye contact with me and motioned that I should come over to his bed. I took it as a signal. I went over to his bed, and I ended up sucking his dick that night. Afterward, we started making out. I probably sucked his dick only twice, but each time we were alone, we had this thing, and we'd make out and masturbate.

IT TOOK A WHILE FOR ME TO REALLY ACT ON MY EMOTIONS.

All this time, Hank and I never talked about what we were doing in those hotel rooms.

I don't know if it was related to what was going on with Hank, but it was around this time that I started getting disillusioned with diving. I wanted to quit. I had felt bad about diving for a very long time and I'd talk a lot about how much I hated it. But I'm not a confrontational person, so it took a while for me to really act on my emotions.

"I'm over diving," I told my mom for what must have been the thousandth time. "I'm over it and I don't want to do it anymore."

On the thousandth time, she finally heard me.

So one day, she drove me to practice and told me if I wanted to quit, I needed to tell my coach myself. I got out of the car and went into the pool area just like on any other normal night of practice. I found Misha, and in front of all my teammates, I told him I needed to talk to him. It wasn't easy. Remember, he was a hard Russian guy. We walked away from everyone and had a private mini-meeting. Everyone who was waiting to train looked up at the office where Misha and I were talking.

I explained to him how much I appreciated his help coaching me over the years, but I wanted to move on with my life. "I don't want to dive anymore," I told him. "I'm formally quitting." He said he knew the day would come. He could see that I was falling out of love with the sport.

In the last few months of my diving career, my mom was sort of the manager of the team. She was the CEO of my diving team. She had become as involved as I was. She would plan competitions and deal with the uniforms, getting sizes for the team, making sure everyone got them on time. The whole bit.

I called my mom the Diving Bitch. Or maybe I just call her that now, though I think she would have loved that name. You've heard of *Dance Moms*? She was Dive Mom. She was a little bit out of her mind.

I know it's hard to imagine, but I really was on the way to the Olympics. The idea of me just deciding to take a different path, of ending that road, of *quitting*—that devastated her. Me quitting the diving team would be as much a life change for her as it was going to be for me.

The thing is, diving was so much of a commitment. It was about to become a profession. The Olympics were everyone's dream and I was on my way there, so maybe it was the pressure. There was so much invested in it because I was good, with a lot riding on my shoulders. Maybe too much. Maybe I didn't want it that much. Diving was taking me away from my social life, and I felt like I was missing out on my childhood. Diving was supposed to be fun, and it wasn't feeling fun anymore.

I also felt ashamed that I quit. I even hated the word *quit.* I'm not a "quitter." I simply didn't want to do it anymore.

Looking back in the rearview mirror of my yellow Mustang, I can't help but wonder if it was also related to the secret relationship that I had going on with Hank. That day I stopped diving, I said goodbye to everyone at the pool. Later that night, Hank and I were talking on MSN Instant Messenger.

ME: "I'm really
sorry it had
to end."

HANK: "It's fine, I
totally get it."

ME: "I'm going to
miss you. All of
our fun travels
and nights in
hotels. All the
memories."

HANK: "I remember."
Wink emoji.
"You wish
I was gay,
don't you?"

ME: "Ummm, yeah."

This is what I remember the conversation being like. I told him I wouldn't be seeing him at diving competitions or really anywhere else.

Me: "I'm really sorry it had to end."

Hank: "It's fine, I totally get it."

Me: "I'm going to miss you. All of our fun travels and nights in hotels. All the memories."

Hank: "I remember." Wink emoji. "You wish I was gay, don't you?"

Me: "Ummm, yeah."

That was it. Sign off, close IM window, go to bed.

A month or two later I ran into Hank at a diving event. I wanted to go and see if there was anything I could help with, since I knew competitions were stressful. Everyone was gagging that I'd quit.

Without really talking about why, Hank and I separated from the group and went out to the playground behind the diving facility. We swung on the swing set side by side and talked about how life had been. My social life had started to bloom since I'd quit, and Hank explained how he didn't want to continue to dive anymore, either. He was looking at colleges he wanted to go to and didn't think diving was the best fit for his life anymore. It was so weird seeing him in the flesh after so long. It almost felt like what we had never existed.

We also talked about how crazy it was that we had done all this "stuff" together. We never articulated out loud what exactly that "stuff" was, but we both knew.

I believe that things definitely happen for a reason.

I'd had a full crush on Hank. And it was brushed under the carpet. Honestly, I know that sounds devastating, but it was fun to have a crush on him. It was easy because we were always together. I don't think I ever thought it was real. I never wanted to really *be* with him. Even then, I think I had a sense of pride about it. The fact that he chose me to hook up with made me feel special because I knew he really liked girls. I've always loved straight guys because of that. I don't even know if I was turned on by the idea of being with Hank. I don't think I wanted to date him.

But, okay, I'll admit it. I felt a little used.

Messing around with Hank was my first real sexual experience. I knew what we were doing was secret and private, but what I remember most was feeling special. Just because it was secret doesn't make it a source of shame. What was important to me was that I got his attention.

It didn't *seem* like that big of a deal, even though it probably *should* have been. Honestly, I would worry about someone else who was describing a similar experience to me. If someone else feels hurt or used by a similar experience, that is one hundred percent legitimate and they need and deserve to receive support and protection. And, looking back, again through that rearview mirror, the difference in our ages seems a little iffy. But I didn't fundamentally feel taken advantage of. I had a part in it. I wasn't passive in the situation, but I definitely wasn't the aggressor, either. I still do sometimes wonder where Hank is and if he's happy.

I don't want to give more power to that experience than it's due. Like, I don't think the relationship I had with Hank stood between me and Olympic gold. Our secret and strange dynamic is not why I quit diving. Looking back, there were so many factors. I wanted a social life and I wanted to experiment with makeup, which ultimately led me toward understanding my true identity. I was trying to become who I am and become comfortable with who I was. I believe that things definitely happen for a reason, and if I hadn't quit diving then, I wouldn't be the person I am today.

If I hadn't quit diving, who would I be? Would I still be Gregory? Would I be Gigi?

But I did quit diving. And I am Gigi.

FAQS

In this book I'm baring my soul to you. I'm telling you every little thing about my life, and it can get a little heavy. But I want to express some of the lighter, brighter things, too. Like some of the questions people ask me all the time. And a few I've never, ever been asked before but are completely illuminating of my sparkling personality.

Are you ready? It's going to be kind of like a speed round.

What's your favorite color?
Baby pink. Because I always have so much trouble picking nail polish colors, and baby pink was what I chose for my very first acrylic set when I was fifteen. What? You thought I'd say shocking pink?

What's your favorite thing about being Canadian?
Canadians are known for being super-nice. And I can be kinda bitchy. So I like that. I'm all about defying expectations.

What are your favorite movies?
The Hot Chick, White Chicks, Mean Girls, and *Titanic.*

Put the Kardashians in order from most favorite to least favorite.

Kim	Kris
Khloé	Kourtney
Kylie	(Sorry!) Kendall

Most important accessory?
A smile. I know it's so cliché. Gross, right? But it's true. Don't forget, I'm Canadian.

Where are your favorite places to go in the world?
1. NEW YORK CITY. I really want to live there one day.
2. TORONTO. I love to visit family when my schedule permits. It's like a mental recharge.
3. BORA BORA. I haven't *actually* been yet, but it looks so turnt.

What are your three favorite clothing brands?

August Getty Atelier, Strike Oil, and Gucci.

What reality shows would you describe as "everything"?

RuPaul's Drag Race. America's Next Top Model (back in the day). *Real Housewives of . . . Beverly Hills, New York City, Orange County, New Jersey. Claws.*

Name a few of your guilty pleasures.

Some of my old favorite TV shows, one being *Gossip Girl*. It's so cheesy, but it's so nostalgic to watch it now. It reminds me of when my friends and I used to binge-watch it after school every day. My other guilty pleasure is being a slob, i.e., not showering after being around the house for a few days and seeing if I can make my burps echo in my house.

Are you a Blair or a Serena (from *Gossip Girl,* duh)?

Blair is more of a villain, so I'm definitely a Serena. I'm blond, innocent, and optimistic like her.

What do you pig out on?

Fast food is life. I've always been obsessed with it. Wendy's. McDonald's. Chick-fil-A. Jack in the Box. Taco Bell. The possibilities are endless.

Do you ever eat healthy?

Yes! Ever since I moved to Los Angeles, I eat a lot more greens and vegan things. I've realized there are more options out here, and everyone is so gnarly about what they eat, so it's kind of made me get into it.

What's your go-to cocktail?

Depends what mood I'm in. A Skinny Margarita when I'm eating Mexican food, Lychee Martini for sushi, Sauvignon Blanc if I'm at a steakhouse, or a Moscow Mule if I can't choose or if I'm already drunk.

How do you deal with the haters?
I literally get asked this *all* the time. Over the years I've been called every name in the book thousands of times over and over again, so it's stopped really affecting me the way it used to. If it's online hate, then I recognize what they're doing, which is going out of their way to type mean things to me and bring down someone they don't even personally know. Something I would NEVER, EVER do. Then I pray for them. Sometimes with my friends. We pray they'll find peace at some point in their lives and learn self-respect and worth. God does the rest.

What's a kind of makeup that changed your life and you couldn't live without?
Mascara. It makes the biggest difference in the shortest amount of time. Without it, my blond lashes make me look like a naked mole rat.

How do you stay so confident?
Ugh, you ask me the most annoying questions sometimes. I'm not always confident. Sometimes I'm a mess and a half. But I've always had a sense of believing in myself and focusing on the good I have in my life. What I've accomplished keeps me motivated, too. Also, surrounding myself with positive people who want the best for me.

What's the highest heel you've ever worn?
A ten-inch stripper heel. It was for this event in New York with my friend and fashion designer August Getty. The custom skirt he made me was so huge, the only way I could navigate with it was by wearing ten-inch heels, or I would've fallen on my face.

What are your tips for wearing super-uncomfortable high heels?
It's so devastating to see a girl walking around without shoes after she's given up on her heels. I keep that image in my mind a lot to get through the night. I also put on a cute look that requires the heels, so without them, the outfit isn't complete, so I absolutely have to keep them on. In other words, I just get into it. And alcohol helps.

If you could go shopping with any celebrity, who would it be?
Britney Spears. I'd love to go to Kitson with her back in the day when it was open. Or I'd love to go to Barneys, turn it out with her and buy everything. There's this one scene in her documentary I've always remembered where she's trying on clothes in a fitting room and being goofy. That is so us.

What do you never leave home without?
My cellphone. My pink pepper spray. Nail glue. And my crew.

What's your worst fear?
Snakes. Like Indiana Jones. (Only thing we have in common.)

What are your top three Britney Spears songs?
So easy. "Anticipating," "Overprotected," and "Toxic."

What's your most played Céline Dion song?
"My Heart Will Go On." My mom and I used to listen to it all the time. She *loved* Céline, which made me love her, too.

What kind of car do you drive and why?
Right now, a 2015 yellow Mustang hard-top convertible. I love it. I personalized it with diamonds on the outside that say my name, and custom racing seats with embroidery. I don't know why I chose it. It just spoke to me. It felt like the perfect first California-girl car, I guess.

2

HOW DO
YOU SAY
"MEAN GIRLS"
IN CANADIAN?

sweet like maple syrup

Gigi wears Make Up For Ever HD Foundation Stick, Tarte Shape Tape Concealer, Anastasia Beverly Hills Brow Pencil, Naicari Solaire Bronzer, House of Lashes Iconic, Becca Topaz Shimmering Skin Perfector Liquid Highlighter, Morphe Dominate Mega Matte Lipstick, MAC Clear Gloss

Like a lot of young gay kids, when I was in elementary school, I had to deal with some classmates who were not so nice to me. Even before I knew what the word really meant, I was the only kid getting called *gay* in my school. And I knew the other kids said it to bring shame on me.

I'd be with girls on the playground jumping rope and other kids would ask me: "Are you gay?" or "Do you want to be a girl?" or "Do you like boys?" And for someone who was hiding who he (or she) was at the time, it wasn't easy to face the truth. These were my deepest secrets. I was all in my head about it, as anyone would be. What was right? What was wrong? Was I gay?

One time I was on the school bus. Maybe it was fifth grade. The cool kids—the eighth-graders—would sit at the back of the bus. On the way home, one of the eighth-graders said to me, "Greg, come back here."

Instantly, I was petrified. This one guy in particular—let's call him Ben—would always make fun of me. The way I spoke, the way I acted, who I was friends with, you name it. He was relentless. I thought, *Oh my God, what is going on? What am I in for?*

I held my head up high and walked to the back of the bus. They were smoking weed. They were so intimidating. Ben held up a magazine. There was a picture of a shirtless guy on the left page and a girl in a bikini on the right. He asked me, "Which one do you like?" They all shoved one another and snickered, waiting for my response.

My entire body got so hot that I went bright red. I was humiliated and embarrassed. I literally wanted to die in that moment. They were all laughing at me. It was awful. The shirtless guy was buff, and, yes, I liked him. Looking over to the page with the girl, I didn't feel a thing.

I thought they could tell everything about me—all my secrets, all the deepest, darkest ones that I didn't even know about myself—just from looking at the expression on my face. After all, they were *eighth*-graders, which at the time seemed like practically adulthood. But before I could fakely point to the photo of the bikini-clad girl, my friend's older sister stood up. She said, "Come on, guys. Stop. Don't do that." I couldn't believe it. She stopped them right in their tracks. And they listened.

Despite the intervention, I felt as if I'd been found out. That people knew who I *really* was. From that moment on, I was terrified every single time I saw Ben or any of his group of bro friends. I couldn't wait for them to graduate and finally leave me alone. The bus ride to and from school was something I dreaded until the end of that year.

But something interesting happened as I started learning who I was. Instead of letting people pick on me, I kind of turned the tables. I started watching out for myself, and sometimes that turned me into a bit of a "mean girl."

Marc was my best friend (and still is). We met in the sixth grade. Like me, he was trying to keep up the "straight" façade, and he's also crazy just like I am. Way back in sixth grade, we made this pact, an alliance, to stick together. It was a conscious effort to be bad. And in a weird way it was kind of like fighting crime for us. Serving justice to whoever deserved it. Like Robin Hood or Spider-Man vibes.

One time at recess, this awful girl called Marc and me "faggots," because of the way we were acting. Now I know she was just trying to be cool. But at the time, she got under our skin.

The day she hurled that insult at Marc and me on the playground, it was raining. For some reason—who the hell knows why?—she was lying down on the ground. So Marc and I picked her up and just swung her into the mud. Full-on crazy. Obviously, violence is never the answer. But here's the thing: She never messed with us or called us "faggots" again. She just went home and changed her clothing and never spoke of what happened.

This other girl in school called us both gay. Let's call her Mary. Mary teased us mercilessly and started a rumor that Marc and I were boyfriends. Well, we didn't get our revenge on Mary immediately. We waited. And one day, sure enough, Mary got her period in class. How did we know? She was sitting two rows ahead of us, and Marc and I saw that she visibly had red on her pants. Yes, it was a shitty thing to do, but why should we keep something like that a secret? No effing way. We let *everyone* know that Mary had her period. We whispered it all around the classroom.

Yeah, that's a traumatizing thing, and she bawled her eyes out. I thought it was just karma. You wrong me, I'll wrong you. Super Regina George.

Later, when I started doing my online videos, I had more of a platform. An outlet. My YouTube channel was well known around the school. Students, teachers, and the head of the school all knew about it and kept up to date with my weekly posts. It made me kind of popular. But that didn't mean I got away scot-free.

For instance, there was this group of girls that didn't like Marc and me because we were loud. They would ask if I was wearing makeup in front of other people, just so I would get embarrassed. They'd call me "cake face" behind my back. I probably was wearing makeup, maybe even too much makeup, but those bitches—I didn't like their *tone*. So whenever there was a school assembly, we would try and sit directly behind them, and we would pull out their flyaways from on top of their heads. Literally pluck hairs out, and they would scream.

Honestly, these people weren't deserving of the abuse, but it's just what we did to survive. High school can be an awful place and kids can be cruel. I just wanted to be bad as a teenager. I had all this strange energy building inside me and I needed to get it out. Lashing out was the easiest way to do so.

Some of my issues were with boys, too.

This one kid—let's call him Stephen—came up to me in art class with this long cardboard pole and he started humping me aggressively. He was doing it really hard and it was hurting me. He was crazy, his hormones running loose in his teenage mind. I was bothered but also confused by it. I barely knew he was in my art class, and we never spoke.

Marc explained to me that what he had done was sexual harassment. I didn't care what it was. I felt violated and I knew it was time for my sweet pay-back. I ended up going to the principal's office to report what he'd done, and Stephen got suspended. Looking back, I actually handled things appropriately that time. Maybe I was growing. Anyway, after that, his group of friends was super-scared of me. Which I liked.

Stephen and I never spoke until recently. I was visiting Toronto and a bunch of my friends and I went to dinner and we saw him. We made eye contact and he came over to our table. He apologized for what he did to me in art class all those years ago. I was shocked.

"It still bothers me to this day what I did to you. I hope you can find it in yourself to forgive me," he said, standing at the head of the table in front of all of my friends.

"It's fine. I can't believe you even remember that. I appreciate it," I replied.

"I think about it all the time," he confessed.

That story may have a satisfying ending, but it's not like my behavior didn't come back to me. That I didn't get my just deserts, if that's what you want to call it.

For instance, I got some major karma in seventh grade. One day, I was wait-ing to get something signed by the teacher and there was a long, slow queue. I don't know why in the hell I had to get this thing signed, but everybody did. It was a school policy or something.

Still, I really had to pee. But I wasn't supposed to get out of line. I asked if I could go to the bathroom, and the teacher running the signing station told me

I could not be excused. I mean, what? Bitch? No. Why couldn't she excuse me to go to the bathroom? But for whatever reason, she just wouldn't. And I didn't just walk out and go. I mean, this was an emergency.

So I pissed my pants. No joke. I was soiled. There was so much pee. It trickled down my denim jeans and onto the ground. Everyone knew. I wanted to go home after that, but the school wouldn't let me do that, either. It was definitely one of my absolute most embarrassing moments ever, ever, ever. Did I mention ever? For all eternity? And I've had some embarrassing shit happen. I mean, who pisses themselves in seventh grade?

YOU NEED TO HAVE YOUR OWN BACK.

It's not like I was fighting my way through high school day in and day out. Marc and I were more into the idea of self-preservation. We knew that we were different. People told us so all the time. We were two of four gay guys in our school. And maybe two lesbians. We knew that we didn't want to be bullied. That said, I don't think we were conscious of all the harm we did, and maybe we were just mean. And maybe for some reason we wanted to see others in pain because we had so much pain ourselves. I'll never say what I did was right. I'm not proud of this period of my life. It was a survival mechanism and I wish that high school hadn't been so hard to survive.

I hate to say this, but in a way, our alliance probably saved me. Having Marc as my best friend made me feel like I belonged. Even if I belonged to a crew of assholes, at least I belonged. I had a group of friends and we supported one another. They had my back and I had theirs.

I know that I had these complicated emotions within myself and I *wanted* people to be intimidated by me. Just like I was intimidated by Ben on that school bus. I wanted people to feel the way he made me feel that day.

I don't think that making fun of people is ever okay. I do think it's important to fight for yourself, to stand up for yourself and what you believe in. It's great to have a thick skin and let things roll off your back, but it's also important to have boundaries, to be able to tell someone that what they're doing is not okay. If someone does something bad to you, there's a time and a place to let it go. But a lot of times, especially in school, growing up, you have to do something or it will keep happening. You need to have your own back. I wish I had used my words instead of reacting physically, but I'll never apologize for having my own back. And the most important takeaway is that you should always do your best to surround yourself with people who love you and support you in what you want to do. That's what Marc was for me, even if from the outside we looked like the obnoxious kids.

I was struggling with another problem in those years, one that came from diving. When I was diving, I was in chlorine all the time, and the chlorine dried out my skin like crazy. I'm already extremely fair, and I have very sensitive skin. On top of that, I was going through puberty, so my oil glands were overproducing, too, which meant my skin basically had no idea what was going on.

Oil glands. That just sounds disgusting.

This meant I had acne. Everywhere. My forehead. My back. My chest. My chin. It was horrible. It was out of control.

People at school would bring it up to me like it was some kind of normal thing to say to another human being. "Oh my God, your skin looks really bad today, you should go wash your face," they'd say. Which is not the thing you want to hear when you're feeling sensitive about your skin. It made me really insecure—and this was a level of insecure on top of the insecure I already felt for just being a gawky, uncomfortable teenager.

And remember, the kids at school were saying this when I was clothed. They had no idea what was going on underneath my T-shirt. I actually made a point to never change in the locker room with the other boys. This wasn't because I was uncomfortable changing in front of them, but because of the terrible acne all over my body. When I was diving, I basically had to be naked, so my insecurity was even worse then. I had to be fully exposed. I'd imagine my teammates and other divers at competitions waiting behind me in line to dive, staring at the hundreds of pimples on my back. Which—I'm sorry in advance for this visual—turned from a pinky red color to a bluish purple because of the cold air in the facility.

The skin problems led, in part, to my makeup obsession. I was always concerned about the redness of my skin, which bullies would point out whenever I got embarrassed in public. Intense acne *and* red skin? No, thank you.

In ninth grade I was dating a girl named Magda (don't worry, I'll tell you more about that "relationship" later). She was surprisingly supportive of my love of everything beauty. One day after school I gave her money to go to the store and buy me makeup. She complied and bought me a product that helped me to cover up some of the problems. It gave me a bit of bravado and definitely made me look better. I had to be careful with it, though, because I didn't want everyone knowing that I was actually wearing it. It was my security blanket when I was out in public, but as a diver, I couldn't wear it in the water. I'd wear the makeup to school, and then I'd clean it off and go to practice at night.

Makeup was my security blanket.

My confidence really suffered because of my skin problems. The acne made me feel bad about myself. It would stop me from talking to certain people at school, and I would always get anxiety whenever I had to talk in front of my class. Or I'd just get embarrassed and I'd feel myself flush up, and then I'd feel doubly embarrassed.

"Oh my God, you're so red" was one of the worst things anybody could say to me at the time.

I knew that I wasn't the only teenager in the world suffering from bad acne and blushing problems. But even though some of my own friends had skin problems, it wasn't something I talked about. I didn't talk about how hard it was for me to deal with. I didn't think anyone had it as bad as I did, so, out of shame, I kept the way I felt about it a secret. I'd just think to myself, *Thank God I'm not diving at this moment and I'm wearing a T-shirt to cover up my body.*

Marc and me dressed as an angel and a devil.

I went to doctors to try to fix it. We tried lots of topical creams, but they didn't work for me. When I was fourteen, a doctor prescribed me Accutane, a pill you take once a day. My dermatologist was reluctant to put me on this treatment at my age, but I couldn't have been more excited. I was on it for almost two years. It really worked, though it was a long process. My eyes, my lips, my ears, my hands—*everything* was gnarly dry for a very long time due to the medicine. This is not a hashtag ad, but I felt extremely free when the Accutane finally cleared up my acne. One day I was like, "Wow. I have absolutely no pimples on my whole body. This is really working."

And the clearer skin happened to dovetail with my coming to terms with my sexuality and coming out. Getting rid of my skin problems, I had a lot more confidence in myself. Without the baggage of having so many pimples, I could focus on something else. I could let go of some of my emotional baggage and move closer to where I wanted to be. One step closer to becoming Gigi.

ICONS I
DIE FOR

Everyone has people who inspire them.

Some of them might say those people are teachers, or coaches, or siblings, or Mother Teresa, or Marie Curie, or Amelia Earhart, or politicians, or trans activists, or whomever the latest turnt scoop du jour of an actress happens to be these days.

Mine include Elisha Cuthbert and Ariel, the Little Mermaid. When I was young, I saw them as guides to how I lived life. How I interacted with the world. How I put together a look. How I acted when I was with people I loved, and how I acted when I was with strangers.

It's not easy to get on my list of inspirational icons.

MINE INCLUDE ELISHA CUTHBERT
AND ARIEL, THE LITTLE MERMAID.

Like I don't have any problems with Rachel McAdams. I mean, I love *Mean Girls*. And, besides, Rachel is Canadian. But a lot of people are in *Mean Girls*— Lindsay Lohan, Tina Fey, and Lacey Chabert among them. And Canada is a huge freaking country. And do I wake up in the morning and think, *Today I'm going to use Rachel McAdams as my spirit guide?* As in: I'm going to dress like Rachel McAdams. I'm going to channel Rachel McAdams when I order my quadruple-shot skim latte at Starbucks. I'm going to think about *The Notebook* when I pose for that fifteenth selfie of the day. I'm going to wonder how much energy Rachel McAdams would get from the energy drink I shouldn't be throwing back into my throat at midnight.

No, absolutely not.

Although I do kind of want to watch *The Notebook* again, ASAP. After all this talk of high school, I'm in the mood for a good cry.

But do I sometimes do that with Sailor Moon, who's on this very curated list you're about to sink your hopefully well-manicured fingers into?

Hundo P.

Elisha Cuthbert

You definitely know who she is even if you don't recognize her name. She was in the movies *House of Wax* and *Girl Next Door.* She's been on a hundred television shows. *Happy Endings. 24.* Some random series with Christian Slater called *The Forgotten* I just looked up on IMDb. But she is Canadian.

And when I was growing up, she was also on this Canadian television show called *Popular Mechanics for Kids,* which I used to watch every single day before I went to school. The young actors on this show would go on spaceships and do experiments and stuff, but from a kid's perspective. It was her and this guy. I don't know where the guy is right now, but I don't really care about him. This is about Elisha Cuthbert. Because I was obsessed with her. And I wanted to look like her. Did I mention she's Canadian? She was this blond, gorgeous bombshell, and she was my beard. You know how gay guys have girlfriends and call them their "beard"? Well, she was the background on my computer screen. I really was consumed with her, but deep down, I wanted to look just like her.

Lady Gaga

She's epic. She actually does it more for me now than she ever has before. Because now she's more real.

When I was in high school, around the time that I started wearing makeup, her album *The Fame Monster* was my everything. You could not compare it to anything else. I saw three concerts of that tour. I loved her crazy outfits. At that time, she was almost not a person to me. She was a mystical goddess of fashion and over-the-top glamour.

I used to wear crazy outfits like her. If she was wearing black lace gloves, I would order them

You "left me speechless."

from Forever 21. I got "left me speechless" as a tattoo. One of the first little movies I made was a video to "Speechless," which I watch every once in a while, because I can't believe I actually did it. But Gaga is that inspiring. I feel like she's just unapologetic about being yourself, about being authentic.

One time I was presenting at the American Music Awards in L.A. and she came up to me during a commercial break. She tapped me on the shoulder and said I looked beautiful. That's honestly the one time in my entire life I didn't know what to say. I was completely and utterly gagged for words. Best moment ever.

Céline Dion

My mom adored Céline Dion and Ricky Martin. I love Céline Dion, too, but not more than my mom did. Along with being wildly talented, I just think she's really extra, and I find it funny. And she's Canadian, so we're proud. I've never seen her in concert, but I really want to. I don't even know what I would do if I met her. It would be such a moment because I know my mom would have wanted to. I probably would be freaked out. I'd totes be starstruck. I probably would be just ridiculous. And now that she's upping her fashion game she's a fashion icon to me, too.

Marilyn Monroe

She's kind of a new one. Don't judge. I like her because she's a blond bombshell, obviously, but I became more obsessed with her when I watched her act in *Gentlemen Prefer Blondes.* The way she moves and speaks was very interesting to me. She oozes femininity. Ever since I moved to Hollywood, I've gotten more obsessed with old Hollywood glamour. Originally I didn't think she was even that beautiful. But now that I watch her on-screen, I see what everyone's gagging about. I also love *How to Marry a Millionaire.* Good advice for all of us!

Sailor Moon

Should I be embarrassed at how much I used to love Pokémon? Don't answer that. But I also loved *Sailor Moon.* I used to watch it so much. It took place in an alternate universe, and Sailor Moon is basically this schoolgirl who wore really short skirts, a schoolgirl outfit, and she fought crime. Kind of like a really dope, sexy anime Catwoman. She had moons in her hair, a tiara, and huge cartoon eyes. She was just a really, really skinny blonde and has turned out to be a major fashion inspiration for me. I love the whole Asian *kawaii* cuteness vibe. The eyes and the colors, the whole aesthetic. Why has no one thought of turning me into a cartoon yet? Hey, that's a great idea. Somebody get on it.

Amanda Lepore

She was brought to my attention by my friend Kyle, who lives in New York. When I first saw pictures of Amanda, I didn't even think she was real. I thought she looked crazy. I thought she was

Photoshopped or looked like a blow-up doll. I met her one night with Kyle at her house in New York. She's exactly what I thought she'd be. A five-foot-two, gorgeous, unrealistically hourglass-framed girl. But in the time we've spent together, I've learned she's very real, and she has a sense of humor and is crazy. She's *funny.*

She was my first real-life tangible example of what a transgender girl was. But her look is so extreme that even if she wasn't transgender, she'd still be a "freak" to some people in society. She's like a showgirl. Very burlesque like Dita Von Teese. If she's like an old Hollywood glamour showgirl, I'm the modern-day Barbie. Though I'm not inspired by Barbie, I had Barbies growing up. But I never died over them. I do, however, die over Amanda. I saw her recently and we laughed our asses off. We were at this club and speaking in really deep voices in each other's ears and then backing up and posing all cute. It was so funny to us we couldn't stop laughing.

Ariel

I love the Little Mermaid. You know, Walt Disney's Ariel. She's so beautiful. I absolutely love the way the movie was done. I must've watched it five thousand times. I love the way she looks. Ultrafeminine. Gorgeous. Innocent. The va-va-voom to her. I was always obsessed with the water as a child, so I related to that. I was always so comfortable in the water. I love when she sings "Part of Your World" and bursts out of the ocean. I used to draw her a lot, too.

If we're speaking freely—and when do I not speak freely?—I think I loved her subconsciously because she had a tail instead of any genitals. I mean, of course she was a girl, but just seeing a tail there kind of felt comforting in a way. A lot of trans people actually relate to mermaids, too. They don't have a penis or a vagina. They're magical beings. And Ariel is the most beautiful mermaid I've ever seen.

Baby Spice

I was, like, six years old, and my dad bought me tickets to my first concert ever. He amped up this gift to me. "You're gonna freak out your guts," he said. "You're gonna die." All right, he probably didn't say exactly that, because who says "You're gonna die" to a six-year-old? But that was the sentiment. And maybe I was seven. Who cares? That's not the point.

They were Spice Girls tickets for a show in Orlando, Florida. I lost my mind. I went with my mom. My first cassette was a Spice Girls album, and I was a humongous fan. My mom probably dropped a hint, or maybe my dad heard me listening to the music. Or saw me watch their movie a thousand times. Whatever. At the concert we were VIPs, with great seats close to the stage. It was a splurge. And I freaked my six-year-old mind out.

Baby Spice wasn't necessarily my favorite Spice Girl at first. I thought Sporty Spice was the best. She was the tomboy of the group. I loved her outfits. And I still do. Because who, at heart, is not most comfortable in a tracksuit? Exactly. Everyone loves a tracksuit.

But I loved Baby Spice because she was the blonde. Yes, I love blondes. And her look! Her look was extremely girly. She was precious, dainty, feminine. *Extremely* feminine (noticing a theme?).

Anyway, I remember the concert vividly, although I don't remember now if it was really in Orlando, or how old I was. But I was living my best life. Even at six or seven, I knew how to do that. I was standing up out of my seat, screaming along with the lyrics, and I turned around and there was a kid around the same age as me with blue hair, slumped down in his seat. He didn't care about the Spice Girls at all! He was probably dragged there by his sister. I remember thinking, *What the hell is this little boy doing? Is this kid ill? I don't understand why he's not dancing.* I didn't get how anyone couldn't love them as much as I did. I'll always remember his face. But I'll also remember Baby Spice's.

Esmeralda

Look, I'm not a Disney freak, okay? I just like a few of the characters. This one's from *Hunchback of Notre Dame,* and I guess if I'm really looking at myself in the rearview mirror of my yellow Mustang, I'll say that this is a movie about an outsider, and that's probably why I liked it so much. And Esmeralda sings a song called "God Help the Outcasts." Go listen to it right now if you need a good cry. Obviously, if you were talking to the sensitive me, I would say I loved Esmeralda because she saw the Hunchback—what the hell was his name? Oh, yeah, Quasimodo—for who he truly was. And I've always wanted people to see me for who I truly am. A cold-hearted bitch. Kidding!

When I was a kid, I used to draw a lot. (See the above entry on Ariel. I drew her, too.) My mom would buy me binders and binders of tracing paper. And my favorite thing to trace was Esmeralda.

People would look at my finished drawings and say, "Oh my God, you're an amazing drawer." I didn't tell them I traced it.

I had *no clue* that Esmeralda was really a thief, but I lo-o-o-ved her. I just thought she was a gypsy who was doing what she needed to do in her village. But really she was stealing things all the time. I was really into stealing once, too. I'll go into more depth shortly, but I started stealing in ninth grade. So I related to that.

And, meanwhile, Esmeralda is *gorgeous.* She's ultrafeminine, which has always been something I've been attracted to either in myself or in others. And I loved how she dressed. She wore little crop tops with her belly showing. Come to think of it, that would make a great Halloween costume. I can be Esmeralda, and let's make my fiancé Nats, the Hunchback. That would be awful. But maybe we should do it.

3

---◆---

STEALING

---◆---

the most is never enough

Gigi wears a Fashion Union jumpsuit, a Kangol cap,
Naicari Rosé Solaire Blush, MAC Studio Fix Powder,
Givenchy Rock N Rose #5, Becca Moonstone Highlighter,
The BrowGal Eyebrow Pencil, MAC Fascinating Eye Kohl

So I was just talking about these skin problems that got in the way of assuming my rightful place as queen of high school, and I started using makeup to help cover up my acne and redness. I told you that I gave money to my first ever girlfriend, Magda, to buy me my first makeup, and that's true. I wouldn't lie to you, bitch!

But there's more to the story of how I began acquiring my amazing collection of beauty products. And there's more to the story of Magda, obviously.

I started stealing in ninth grade. And I don't mean a pack of gum from the convenience store here and there. I mean stealing on the regular. It got really bad. It was one hundred percent an addiction.

This might be harder for me than it is for you, but picture me at the time. I was plain old Gregory. Gay, but not out of the closet. Yet. A really big MySpace user. Super into the emo look. Terrible skin.

Plus, throw in some bangs and eyeliner. It kind of sounds depressing, right?

Well, add this into the mix. So when I say I was "dating" Magda, I mean we would talk a lot. We would sort of kiss once every week. Like a peck here and there. Not on the mouth or anything. No. Never on the mouth.

I would lie to her about all the sexual things I wanted to do to her. But I never really got around to doing those things. Basically, we'd just talk about them. And I'd delay them and delay them because I knew I didn't want to do any of those things with her.

But we had a lot of things in common. We were both on MySpace. We were both into the "scene" look. We were really into rock bands where guys would wear makeup. And, together, we started stalking these Internet celebrities, like Jeffree Star, Christina Dolce—who was nicknamed ForBiddeN—and Tila Tequila.

The day came in our relationship when I felt comfortable enough to tell her that . . . I wanted to start straightening my hair. It would be an homage to those Internet celebrities we liked so much. But I couldn't buy a hair straightener on my own. Why it was such a big deal, I don't really know now. But going into the store to buy my own hair straightener seemed like such an ordeal. A to-do. Something so embarrassing. And because I had hidden so much of my identity from the "real world," I didn't want to be seen buying something "girly."

So I gave Magda money, and I asked her to get me a hair straightener.

One thing led to the next and I started asking Magda to get me makeup. I couldn't buy my own makeup, I thought. No, I definitely couldn't do that. She was literally my dealer.

I went to the CoverGirl website to pick out some things that would work for me. I color-matched my foundation on the screen and picked out a few shades of blush and lipstick that I thought I'd like. I told her I wasn't comfortable getting it myself, so I gave her money to go get it. Once a day, she would go to the store, and she would come back with new makeup for me to try out.

I wasn't getting enough makeup that way, so I started stealing my mom's makeup. She had only twenty or thirty things in her collection. Maybe to you that sounds like a lot, but it wasn't enough for me. She wasn't a makeup fiend. Plus, taking her makeup meant I would get in trouble with her, too. She started to catch me "borrowing" her makeup and wondered why certain things of hers had traveled all the way over to my room and hadn't exactly traveled back.

I was embarrassed to buy my own makeup. That act of just bringing the makeup up to the counter and turning over my debit card to pay for it was too much for me at the time. So to avoid that moment when I was confirming for the world that I, Greg, was buying makeup, I ended up stealing makeup from the drugstore instead. It was easier emotionally, less invasive, I guess. And it was also kind of a thrill. I have an addictive personality, so when I like something, I really want it all. I wanted to amass the biggest makeup collection. Some of the other things I've been addicted to (or remain addicted to) are:

- people (if I like somebody, I just always need to be around them)
- social media
- cute animals
- drinking and partying
- Facetune

- fame
- traveling
- love
- vanity
- spending money (which comes up later in the chapter, you'll see)

The first thing I stole was at this place Sally's Beauty Supply, which was literally down the street from school. I was with Magda. She went in to buy hair dye. When she was checking out, I went to the back and put a bottle of Bed Head After-Party, which is a kind of leave-in conditioner, into my backpack. It came in a hot-pink bottle. I'd seen it online and I'd always wanted it. I think it was $30, and I had only $20 on me, and at the time, I didn't have a debit card, either.

Okay, I'll stop making excuses—I freaking wanted to steal it.

I didn't tell Magda I took it. I just got away with it. Maybe because it was the first thing I ever stole, it became one of my favorite products ever.

These days, I'm super used to having makeup around all the time, but in high school, I wasn't. I was addicted to makeup and I was addicted to stealing. I made this weird, indescribable pact in my head: That I was going to steal every day for an entire year. It was some kind of insane promise to myself.

I have no idea why I did this. Has anyone ever made a pact in their head like that? To steal every day for a year? It's fucked! And *not* the good "fucked"! Though at the same time, I'm kind of like, what kind of badass was I at the time? Who did I think I was? A part of the Suicide Squad? Also what kind of idiot, that I thought it was a good thing to steal every day for a year?

I was stealing hair straighteners, expensive luxury makeup, luxury skincare, you name it. I stole everything. Stealing was my thing. Obsessed with it. Some of these things came in big boxes. I have no idea how I hid and hauled everything out, but I did. My mom would often come into my room and ask where I was getting all this new stuff from. I'd usually say I bought it, but sometimes I'd say they were gifts.

"Pretty nice gifts . . ." she would answer.

I wouldn't lie to you, bitch!

Stealing was a rush to me, more about the feeling than the thing I was stealing. I fucking loved it. I could compare it to a drug, it was so addictive. I would literally be itching to go to the mall. The thing is, at a certain point, I had the money to buy these things because my YouTube channel started to take off at the same time my makeup collection was taking off. But I just *wanted* to steal. I think it was a hobby, to be honest. A strange, strange hobby that also involved truly building my makeup collection.

I stole so much makeup right until the time I got caught. I stole from MAC Cosmetics. It was at the mall right by my house, Square One. I knew so many of the girls who worked there. They kind of became my friends. I really looked up to them like big sisters. And funny enough, one of them was named Kim, which was the name I had insisted on being called by my brothers when I was very young. Whenever I got paid, that was the first place I would always go to spend my money. But even though I'd buy things there, it was also part of my stealing ritual. I'd go and buy something so I'd already be carrying a bag from MAC, and then I'd leave the store and go shop somewhere else. I'd come back and sneak a tester or something into my bag.

But on this one day, I came back to MAC with a bunch of other shopping bags. I sneaked a tester of foundation and a few other items from the counter. The girls at the store weren't talking to me like they always did, so I knew something was off. I decided to get out of there. On my way out, there was a cop at the front door waiting for me.

"You need to give back what you stole," he said firmly.

He made me prove what I'd actually bought that day, checking all of my receipts individually. Of course, I couldn't prove some items. So he handcuffed me. As I was standing outside that store, a few of my subscribers walked by and saw me. People from my school did, too. It was absolutely humiliating. But it was a big wake-up call.

After two hours of intimidating me, the cop told me that I wasn't going to get in trouble, but I would be blacklisted from the mall. My picture was going to go up on the wanted list. I wasn't supposed to go back there for a year.

I went back to the mall after like a month, though, because I'm that bitch. I didn't go visit the girls at the MAC store. I was so embarrassed. I remember we saw each other through the glass windows when I walked by. It was so awkward. I had trouble confronting them. I found the idea of going in there to apologize difficult because I betrayed their trust. Anyone would feel ashamed, but apologizing would have been the right thing to do. I was just being a stupid teenager.

BUT I JUST *WANTED* TO STEAL. I THINK IT WAS A HOBBY, TO BE HONEST.

I totally had an addiction to material things. I could buy this stuff, but it was more of a thrill to *take* it. Part of stealing was that it gave me the opportunity to impress people. Whenever I would steal in front of my friends, it was kind of exciting. I would get a shock out of them. "What do you want me to steal for you, girl?" I'd say.

"How did you get away with that?" they'd say. "Where did you hide it?" I felt so much pride that I would get away with it time and time again.

Maybe stealing was an outlet to escape what I was really feeling, too.

There was a lot more going on in my head than I could have even imagined. I was definitely suppressing my thoughts about being transgender. I knew I was gay, yes, but I wasn't totally happy in my gay identity. I knew something else was going on with me. I would see all the kids in my school as super-happy, even if deep down they might have been confused like I was. I saw everyone else as "normal" and myself as messed up in a way. They'd have boyfriends and girlfriends, and I felt like I'd never have something "normal" like that. And all of that made me so angry. Stealing allowed me to take my anger out on something else.

Well, I guess it's no surprise that Magda and I didn't work out. We ended up separating. I was spending my time stealing and YouTubing anyway. I came out of the closet right after we broke up. I don't even know if we had a conversation about it. During that period, I was lying about so much, I think it allowed me to be fake with Magda, too. I still worry that I hurt her by allowing her to think that I was interested in a way I wasn't. I was so immature that I hardly lingered over the end of the relationship. Instead of being obsessed with the breakup, I was obsessed with makeup.

Somehow, though, while I was hiding so much about my identity, confused about who I was, and also literally hiding hauls of stolen products in my room, I was also kind of outed by my increasingly obvious love of makeup. Even though I had not come out publicly, I think that all my real friends knew that I was a gay boy. How could they not? Then again, people called me gay in the schoolyard at recess before I even knew what it meant. The inflection of the word and the laughter that followed were intended to remind me that it wasn't "normal" to be gay.

I always loved that I was gay. I always knew that it made me unique. But I also knew that no one else in my family was gay, and in that very stereotypical way, I worried that it would bring my family shame. That they would all be embarrassed of me if they actually knew the truth. That's the kind of attention I learned to avoid, and I wanted it to stay that way.

So I turned fifteen without my parents knowing I was gay. At that point, it was really weighing on me. I knew that I had to tell them. My parents had a second home in upstate New York, several hours from where we lived. We used to go skiing there every single weekend in the winter. My mom made sure of it. It was our family bonding time.

One random weekend I was in my bedroom and I was chatting online with my friend Zachariah, who lived in New York and was gay and out to his family. My brothers were watching television behind me and my parents were downstairs. Part of me was angry that I couldn't have my own social life. That I had to come on these annoying family weekends without my friends. That I couldn't be independent. My parents would always tell me to bring my friends, but none of them skied, and I felt like it would be boring for them.

Basically, Zachariah convinced me that there was no time like the present. That I should talk to my parents. "Fuck it," he said. "Just do it. It won't be that bad." I thought, *He's right. Fuck it.* I wrote "BRB" to him on the computer.

I felt really emotional, but I knew that I had to do it. Everyone reaches their breaking point, and this particular weekend was mine. I loved them, and I wanted them to know the truth about me. I wasn't going to pretend anymore to be something I wasn't.

I got to the ground floor of the house and freaked out. I hovered in the kitchen, where my mom and dad were cleaning things up. I was so nervous. I fumbled around, not knowing what to do with myself, out of fear of starting the conversation. A total eek-a-deek.

I said to my mom and dad that there was something that I'd been wanting to tell them. We sat down in the living room within earshot of my brothers and I said the two hardest words I had ever had to say up until then: "I'm gay." And the second I said it, my mom starting crying. I think she knew I was going to say it. She wasn't crying because she was upset or—my biggest fear—embarrassed, but because she was scared for me, scared about the people in the world. Scared, that I could get hurt physically, or even murdered for it. My father, on the other hand, handled it like a businessman. He was extremely strong and nurtured both my mom and me. They were both thankful that I had opened up to them about something so personal. And my mom confirmed what I had always thought: She did already know I was gay. I often wonder if in that moment she even knew I was transgender. They both hugged me and said they would always love me no matter what.

When I got back upstairs to my computer, I told Zachariah what I'd done. He was so supportive. "Congratulations! Doesn't it feel so much better?" he asked me. And yes, it did. I felt so much better after. I felt free. This was the first time that I'd really gone against the mold, that I'd really realized something about myself and was able to say it out loud. My brothers already knew

I was gay, but they overheard the entire conversation and congratulated me as well.

I went to bed that night so happy. I fantasized about coming out to the entire world. At that point, Marc, Zachariah, my brothers, and my parents were the only people who knew that I was gay. Over the next few months, I told everyone in my life. Then, about a year later, I made a coming-out video for YouTube and told the world. Or at least the world that cared about watching my YouTube videos.

After I came out to them, I think my parents saw they needed to give me more independence. They saw that I was more mature. That I was less tortured about my friendships and my relationships with them and with my brothers. That a lot of my anger had gone away. I wasn't quite as petulant, I guess, is the word for it.

The truth was, my parents shouldn't have really been worried or upset about me in the first place. Yes, I know. They couldn't control other people and what they thought. They couldn't control the world around me. They couldn't control the kids who would be mean to me.

Little did they know I was going to be just fine. It wouldn't matter if I was the queen of my high school or not; I was going to become an Internet sensation.

It wouldn't matter if I was the queen of my high school or not; I was going to become an Internet sensation.

SAY MY NAME, SAY MY NAME:

JUST CALL ME GORGEOUS

I know you've all seen every single one of my YouTube videos and have watched my documentary *This Is Everything* at least three times.

And if you haven't, well, W-w-w-wait. That's shocking. It's actually kind of awesome that you're reading this without any prior knowledge of who I am. Or with just a little bit of prior knowledge, whatever the case may be.

Regardless, I guess we should start at the very beginning. And that would be when I was born a boy, named Gregory Allan Lazzarato, in Montreal, Quebec.

And then let's jump ahead a few years. To when I created my YouTube channel.

There was a lot of pressure around figuring out a name for my YouTube channel. I was always changing my Instant Messenger name because that was totes easy and I had nothing else to do, but there was this idea that, with YouTube, once you came up with your channel name, you could never go in and change it. I knew that from the beginning, and I didn't want to make my channel until I had my name.

I knew that I wanted to create a brand. See? Even then, as a somewhat stubborn Canadian boy teenager, I had foresight. Isn't that turnt? Who do you think you're talking to, anyway? And I knew I wanted my YouTube handle name to be a person's name. I didn't want it to be called GlitteryMakeup18 or JuicyGloss9, like a lot of the other girls online were doing. I didn't want it to be called Stars and Rockets. I wanted it to be dope.

My MySpace name at the time was Gregory Graves. That's how long ago this was, and how new being a YouTuber was. There was still MySpace!

Gregory Graves was just an emo look. It was not my life or who I really was at all. I was basically trying to fit in with the MySpace kids. I didn't listen to screamo music. I wasn't a scene kid. I just saw people online living like that and I thought I would try to fit in with them. A lot of people liked the repeat-the-letter thing.

It's catchy, right? I just Googled it and it's called "alliteration." So I did that, too.

But "Gregory Graves" was not going to fly for a YouTube channel about makeup. Unless I was going to be doing makeup for dead people at funeral homes or something. I guess that's called embalming. And it's also called a little bit gross because a) I can't and b) I won't.

My friend Marc was in my ear. He was the one suggesting that I do this whole YouTube thing anyway, and I think he even used the word *gorgeous* to describe me when he introduced me to other people. Although I don't think I felt gorgeous when I started out, but that's okay. Sometimes it's about *learning* to feel gorgeous.

Gorgeous meant beautiful, and that's how makeup made me feel. I felt gorgeous when I was done up. I felt different. Gorgeous was about knowing your self-worth. And that's how Gregory Gorgeous was born.

And then eventually I got my name Gigi. Gregory Gorgeous = GG. Get it? That's the abbreviation. And GG sounds like Gigi. Some people would even call me

Gigi when I started to look more feminine, anyway. It was kind of like a nickname that just stuck. When I started to transition, I changed Gregory Gorgeous to Gigi Gorgeous. Easy as that.

Something a lot of people ask me, as well as other people in the trans community, is how trans men and women get their new names. The names they weren't born with. That's a big question. Mine was literally and fully created organically. I didn't pick it out of thin air.

Legally, my name is now Gigi Loren Lazzarato. A lot of people think "Loren" comes from Sophia Loren. But, really, my mom was going to name me Lauren if I had been born a girl (which she totes thought I was going to be). I just wanted to put my own little twist on it. I thought it would be a genuine tribute to her even though she never got to meet me as Gigi.

Getting my name change was a total gag. Actually, it was more of a pain in the ass. I'd wanted it changed for a really long time. And the process to get it changed was way more than I thought it would be. I had to deal with all of this government stuff. I was like a private investigator about it. Things were slow because I had to get my birth certificate. I lived in Toronto, but I was born in Quebec. Those are two different provinces, if you don't speak Canadian, and the translation is that it turned out to be kind of a whole process. It was a *lot* of back and forth.

Not having Gigi as my real name was something that always haunted me, especially because I traveled so much for work. Whenever I would be in airports, I'd be all pretty and done up, because I would always get "ready" before I'd travel. Someone told me once, you never know who you're going to meet at the airport, so always look your best. Something I don't stand by religiously, but, you know, I just heard it one time. But it'd be really embarrassing because I was carrying a passport that said "Gregory" and "male" on it, and if there was ever an issue with my seat, they would always call me up to the lectern in front of EVERYONE. I would always wait a beat, do a circle around the terminal, and come back just to

make sure that people weren't staring.

The truth is, I absolutely cared what people thought. It sucks that I did, but I can't avoid that I did. I can't sugarcoat it. No matter what anyone says about living your truth, it can be uncomfortable and embarrassing in certain social situations. Especially at the beginning. I knew people would read "Gregory" on my passport as I was standing in front of them looking really feminine with my full face and hair done. I just didn't want total strangers to know that I was trans.

After I got my face done—which you'll read about extensively in an upcoming chapter—I remember I came home to my dad's house in Toronto. I still looked a little messed up. I wasn't, shall we say, gorgeous at all, on the outside or inside. I felt like crap. I was miserable. I was really in transition. I had to wear a hat because I had this scar on my head that I had to keep bandaged 24/7.

But when I got home, I found that my name-change documents were there, in the mail on my bed. It was official. I was so excited. I was now, for real, just Gigi Loren Lazzarato. And that meant it felt more and more like I was becoming a woman. Not just a woman, but the person I wanted to be and the person I knew I was inside. It validated me insanely.

G's. I hate when people spell my name like that. I know it was a typo, but it's just not my name. So Adam fixed the cake on his own, and it was really cute seeing him care about my new name. Especially because my older

I was now, for real, just Gigi Loren Lazzarato.

Plus, my older brother, Adam, and my "sister"/his former girl-friend Tiffany got me a cake. It was a white cake with chocolate inside, one of those from the grocery store that you can write whatever you want on top of. Adam had done the writing; I could tell because it wasn't very neat. It said "Congratulations GiGi!" He did it with two capital

brother tends to be really stoic. He doesn't usually talk about his feelings, but he was really supportive. He always made sure to call me "Gigi" and use the pronoun "she." I know a lot of trans girls don't have that kind of love from their family, and it was beyond my wildest dreams that my new identity was on a cake.

4

---◆---

SPENDING

---◆---

because I
earned it

Gigi wears a vintage '60s dress, MAC Boldly Bare Lip Pencil, MAC Crème D'Nude Lipstick, Anastasia Butterscotch Lip Gloss

Another truth is I kind of traded one addiction for another addiction. I had an addiction to stealing, and then, when I started to make money from YouTube videos, I developed a shopping addiction I didn't even realize at the time.

It's funny. My parents were very careful about money. Every week on Sunday after church, we'd get our age in allowance. If I was twelve, I'd get $12. And then I'd get to keep $2, and the rest would go to my savings, which, amazingly enough, I still have.

My mom would only rarely buy anything for my brothers and me unless it was something we definitely, absolutely needed. School uniforms, for instance. She'd never give us random presents. She was never a label whore (which I totes wish she was, because who wouldn't want to rock a vintage Louis Vuitton handbag?). She and my father were careful and protective. They made sure that I knew the value of a dollar.

When I started earning my own money and saw my bank account rising, I just wanted to spend the money. To buy myself things. Lots of things. Tangible things. Things that made me feel like I was successful and accomplished and, maybe, just maybe, better about myself. Did they actually make me feel better? They definitely helped me forget myself and my problems for a moment or two.

When I was sixteen, I used to do huge online-order shopping sprees. Like I'd order a shit ton of clothes for that music video I did of Lady Gaga's "Speechless." You can look it up online. I still live for it.

I loved Forever 21 because it was so cheap. When you order from Forever 21, did you know you can put only fifty items in your cart at a time? You probably didn't. But I did. I was always getting the message: "You have fifty items in your cart. You can't add any more."

One of my first photoshoots in my favorite (at the time) American Apparel dress.

Why the hell did I need fifty things from Forever 21 at a time? Why the hell *didn't* I?

My friend Marc and I were both super-girly, and we would have so much to play with. Boxes and boxes and boxes would come in the mail. Dresses, shoes, accessories, earrings, rings, hats. I'd tell my mom that they were for "projects" I was working on. (Watch Lady Gaga "Speechless" video again. Then rinse, repeat.)

Makeup had come first, but by this point I had fallen in love with girls' clothes. Boy's clothes were *boring*. Girls' clothes just seemed prettier and more feminine. More me.

I had a big closet, but my room was filled with clothes. My mom used to freak out. I had so much shit. My mom would just say, "Look, no more shopping" or "I hope you're saving your money." I was saving some money from my job. Not nearly enough money, but at least I was saving some.

My bathroom was filled with products. I had eighty shampoos and conditioners. Eighty! For no reason. And a hundred things were coming in the mail a week for me. Like a fucking hoarder.

I wasn't wearing girls' clothing to school, but I had a world outside high school where I could go on the weekends. A world where I could be myself, or at least *more* of myself.

When I was a senior in high school, I'd started going to my older brother, Adam's, college to hang out and go to college parties. He invited me because I was fun. I've always been very outgoing and not afraid to meet new people. That was never, ever a doubt.

And a big part of it was my brother's girlfriend Tiffany. Tiffany was and is basically my sister (although she and my brother eventually stopped dating after nine years together). I remember the first time we met. Every week, my dad, my mom, and Cory and I used to go out to visit Adam at college, an hour's drive away. But this time was special. We were meeting in a new restaurant and we were meeting my brother's new girlfriend, Tiffany. *Oh, this is interesting,* I remember thinking. *Let's see what she's all about.*

I LIKED GIRLS' CLOTHES BECAUSE THEY WERE TIGHTER. I HAD TWO BROTHERS, AND TO ME, BOY'S CLOTHES WERE *BORING.*

It turned out, she was so nervous to meet us. She had watched the YouTube videos I posted, including the one where I came out online. She would always quote me and the things I said online because she found them funny. I was a little bit embarrassed, but also just kind of happy. It was validating and nice to know I had that support from her.

But then somehow we started talking and bonding over Céline Dion. Tiffany said her music made her cry. I said, "What do you mean, cry?! I don't remember the last time I cried! You're such a baby!" (This was before hormone therapy cracked open the part of me that's able to cry.) When she went to the bathroom, I went in with her to the girls' room, which was something I did only with close girlfriends at that time. She just totally got me. And that was pretty much the beginning of our forever friendship and sisterhood.

My brother loves our family. He loves seeing me happy and sharing his life, which makes me all warm and fuzzy inside. I think he was also nervous to go

Tiffany and me
clubbing in Toronto

away to university alone, and I think it made him feel better to have me there whenever I could make the trek. And Tiffany and I had so many of the same tastes. We used to watch everything together, from new Nicki Minaj music videos to *The Hills.* And if we weren't in the same city, we'd just text all the livelong day.

So on the weekend, I would go to Adam's school dressed as a version of Gigi, or a pre-version of Gigi. I made friends with Adam and Tiffany's friends, and we would all go out. It was a group of like fifteen of us. Everyone was very supportive, which surprises me even now. It also makes me feel really blessed to have had that at such a young age. Back then, I never questioned myself. Well, that's not a hundred percent true, but I was also more sure of myself than I probably had any right to be. I saw going to his college as a huge party.

Being somewhere other than home also gave me the opportunity to experiment, a safe zone with my brother and his friends. I knew that no one from my high school would be there. They were miles away both geographically and in terms of maturity.

Here, I could wear high heels and be someone else. I could be Gigi, I guess, before I was really even Gigi. I didn't have to worry about the so-called cool kids in high school judging me. I was already "cooler," if there is such a thing.

Was my brother conscious of this? Do I think he invited me on purpose to get me out of my little world? To put me in a place where I would be comfortable to experiment, where I didn't have to worry about being picked on and made fun of? To give me a safe haven to be who I was and who I am?

I like to think that all of those things are true. My brother and I have never really talked about that stuff, so maybe he did it instinctively or unconsciously, without even realizing it. Whether it was on purpose or not, it was great for my self-confidence and self-respect. Though I should tell you, I don't know if I ever really had a problem with self-confidence.

In fact, since I was a child, my whole MO has been trying to make my brother as uncomfortable as possible. I'd show up in the most ridiculous outfit I could, putting those Forever 21 hauls to good use. It was crazy, because his school was in what I like to call Hick Assville. Ever heard of it? Good, because you definitely do not want to move there, or even stop by for a Twisted Mango Diet Coke. Unless you're with me—I'll show you a great time. I know where all the good bars are, don't worry.

The people who live in Hick Assville were not the nicest, most genuine and forgiving people in the world. But when I walked into a room, I made sure they loved it. It was like I was a celebrity. These were college dorms and college bars filled with extremely conservative people. And I'd go dressed up to the nines. The most eye makeup ever. They all kind of just bowed down to me.

I've always seen homophobic people as a challenge to break through. It's like pushing a boundary and breaking a mold. I loved messing with those hick boys and small-minded people alike. Maybe I got called a name or two here and there, but that was to be expected. *Clearly* I was different from everybody else. I'd take it as a victory if there weren't any comments made, which happened more times than not. I never got in serious trouble. This was a safe enough environment where I could mess with the system.

Those days are some of the literal best ones of my life. It was family bonding time, self-expression time, growing-up time, but it was all so much fun. I look back at pictures now and I realize I didn't even second-think what I was doing. I was just *living*. I was beautiful and confident in everything that I wore and how I acted. I truly loved every minute of it.

It was fun to experiment, too. Like I had a stage to perform on, but I also had my brother to protect me in case I were to fail. YouTube was not a thing there. These people didn't necessarily know who I was online or if I was a loser in high school. Basically, I had my sister and brother and a town an hour away where I could go to party. I was a kid but not a kid.

And when I'd go back to my regular high school life, I realized it wasn't the be all and end all of things. I didn't need to take it so seriously. I had more life experience now, and I knew there was a whole world of people out there. So I went to school with more confidence, with more self-love, with stronger bonds to my family. In general, that just made me care less about what other people thought about me. I encourage you to look for an escape where you can express yourself—whether it's dance class, the park, or the football field—so that you can make your life and your reality bigger than it already is.

The truth is, I felt my most popular in high school when I was with my closest friends. Marc, for instance, was my backbone. He would amp me up with a lot of confidence. "No, you're killing it," he'd say, especially at times when I thought I wasn't. The truth is, it's important to remember that no one knows who they are in high school. That's something I can assure you of.

The truth is, it's important to remember that no one knows who they are in high school.

I look back at that time of my life and I'm so thankful that I had (and have) a family that watched over me, who helped me adjust to who I am. I know not everybody has that, and I'm extremely lucky. And if you don't have that, I encourage you to do everything in your power to go out into the world and *find* that family. It's possible, I promise you. I have a family outside of my family that does that for me every day in Los Angeles.

But it's also about trying not to care about what other people think. I don't necessarily think this is an easy task, either, but pushing the envelope a little will help you figure out who you are. And as long as you feel it's a safe enough place, go where you can be you, or at least try a new you on. Trust me, it's the best feeling ever.

It wasn't until the end of high school, when I moved to college myself and had to pack all my stuff, that all the clothing I was hoarding became an issue. That's when my mom realized I'd been stealing, too. She knew there was just no way I had enough money for all that luxury makeup.

She was furious with me. She instantly made me go through everything and pack up what I didn't need (which was about eighty percent of my closet and bathroom) and drove me to a shelter to give it away.

I look back now and realize that, yes, I probably had a stealing and shopping addiction. The ultra-weird thing is that I'm realizing it literally right now, as I write this, for the first time. What was going on then?

I think I was hiding a lot of things. I was a gay boy who loved makeup. I wasn't being honest with and about myself, and hoarding was probably helping me hide that. I was putting my energy into something else rather than into self-reflection.

I'M DEFINITELY SUPER AGAINST THAT CHIP THING ALL THE CREDIT CARD MACHINES HAVE NOW. NO DRAMATIC SWIPE.

But I also used that clothing to literally try on a new identity. I wore it to all those parties where I could emerge as a totally new person—not just Gregory. Maybe I was hiding in the clothing, but it also helped me reveal the person I truly am.

When it comes to shopping now, I go in waves. What can I say? I like the thrill of spending. The *cha-ching* vibes of my credit card. I'm definitely super against that chip thing all the credit card machines have now. No dramatic swipe.

One of my hoarding problems is that as much as I like to buy, I hate to return. So now that I live in Los Angeles, I donate what I'm not using to trans kids who need clothing in my area. That feels like a really good way to turn something I don't necessarily lurve about myself into something that I do.

KISS

AND

MAKE UP

When it comes to my appearance, I'm usually in my own lane. I always had an extreme look: lots of hair, lots of makeup, dramatic clothing. It's what I call "extraness."

I learned a lot about how to put together a look from my mom. From the time I was born she was a housewife, but she also ran a drapery business out of our basement. Even if she wasn't the most fashionable or flashy, when it came to her look, she had a certain confidence. Whenever my mom walked into a room, the party would start. Her laugh was *so* distinct. She loved to laugh. She was blond. She was statuesque. No matter what, she had a kind of star quality.

The first time I put makeup on, I was probably four or five. I was playing with my mom's lipstick after watching her put on makeup. And my Barbies had makeup that you could switch out. But I didn't really seriously put on makeup until I was about fourteen. As I've already mentioned, I started doing makeup to fix my really bad skin. I was also inspired by makeup looks I saw on celebrities, and it made me want to be creative, to see if I could do it myself.

It worked for a while, but I got heavy-handed with it. One thing led to another. Bronzer would lead to blush. People would start to call me out on the fact that I was wearing too much makeup. I guess I found it easier to pretend that I wasn't wearing it at all. My mom would take her thumb to my face and say, "Why are you lying? You're wearing makeup."

My history teacher, Mr. T., was really beautiful. Everyone had a crush on him—even, I'm sure, some of the straight boys. We were friends, and I'd talk back to him. I'd be pretty sassy. One day he looked me in the face and asked me, "Are you wearing bronzer?" I think he thought he was just messing with me, but of course I was wearing bronzer. I said that I wasn't. It really hurt my feelings that he said that.

I lied about this stuff because I wanted people to think I was perfect and had good skin, even though I didn't. It was kind of a dark time. Girls would come up to me and say, "Your skin is everything." Of course I was wearing makeup at the time, so I took these compliments as insults—like, I felt they were trying to pump me up because they knew I had a problem with my skin, or they were just trying to point out that I was wearing makeup. I guess I was just a delusional teenager. Until I started owning up to it on my YouTube channel.

Once I owned it, it wasn't that bad. Just like everything. Here's the real truth: You feel so much better and most certainly more authentic when you just own up to the things that you think it might be too difficult to own up to.

I learned about what kind of makeup to wear from doing lots of research online and from trial and error. If I saw a blond model in a campaign at Shoppers Drug Mart that caught my eye, then I knew to wear that shade. If you're fair like me, the choices are medium beige or ivory; I kind of had the sense that the ivory was probably more my color.

As Gregory, the pretty gay boy, I experimented with different kinds of makeup, in this order: concealer, foundation, bronzer, lip gloss, blush, brow powder, brow gel, clear mascara. Concealer was the gateway drug, I guess.

I progressed to hair extensions. Whenever I did my own hair extensions, it would look kind of busted. Eventually, when my friend taught me how to put them in, they looked much better.

The dead giveaway was always the eye makeup. When I still felt a little unsure of myself, I would always go for the natural, I'm-not-wearing-makeup look. It made me look better, or at least I thought it did, but it didn't make me stand out. Still, when I was Gregory, I yearned to wear mascara.

Putting on mascara was the real turning point. People would notice. They *knew*. They *knew* I was wearing more makeup than I had the day before.

I remember the first morning I wore black mascara. My mom would walk me to the front door every single morning as I left the house to go to the bus. On this morning, she looked at me wearing my perfectly applied mascara.

"You look gorgeous," she said to me confidently. It was such a *moment*.

5

LOSING MOM

was just down the street. On one of those drives, she asked me why I wasn't going to class.

"I'm just not going," I replied.

"Why? Are you not happy?" she asked. Or maybe it was "Why aren't you happy?" I remember it being in the most calming tone.

I didn't know how to answer her.

She still had her long blond hair, but her energy was very low. "If you're telling me you're not going to class, I just need to see it for myself."

It's like it was yesterday. We went to the office of the head of the fashion management program at my school. It was me, my mom, and the registrar at the desk. The registrar pulled out my file and showed my mom my attendance record. I'd been to class a total of ten times over the course of a year and a half. My mom wasn't mad. She didn't scream. She just said that she was going to take me out of the program. She and my dad wouldn't get any money back. That was it. It was over. I was a college dropout.

It was a really bad moment for me. I felt like a complete failure. A failure who was also a spoiled brat. It seemed like I wasn't doing—and couldn't do—anything productive. At that time, to my family, YouTube didn't seem like work. It was my passion, but my mom and dad thought it was just a hobby. I don't think they realized how much I was putting into my channel, or that I was consistently doing brand deals. That I was getting paid $8,000 to talk about a self-tanner. And it was a self-tanner that I actually liked. Kinda turnt.

Maybe if I had told my parents at the time that I was making a living, they would have looked at my college experience differently. They would have seen where I was putting my energy. But I obviously wasn't communicating my feelings. I was dealing with my sense that I was more of a girl than a boy. And I was dealing with my mom slowly dying before my eyes. Little did I know I had less time with her than I could have ever imagined.

My mom wasn't happy with how I fared in college. Even though she was really angry, she didn't punish me. She just said, "We're not going to continue putting you through the next few weeks of school." So I moved back home with my parents and my younger brother, into their house.

Of the three of her kids, I was the one my mom was most open with about her breast cancer. I remember the first time she and my dad told us she had it. They sat us all down in a family meeting after dinner and told us we were all going to do whatever we could to fight it. We knew she was going to look a little bit different because of chemo and radiation, but we as a family unit were ready.

She ended up losing her hair. It was shocking to see my mom without hair for the first time. She had lost a lot of weight and wasn't the same Mom I knew. It felt like she was somewhat ashamed of having cancer. I knew she was frustrated about how the chemo and radiation treatments made her feel. It would wipe her out for a couple days, and then, after a few days of feeling back to normal, she would have to go to the hospital again and get another round. But she ended up beating it the first time around, when the cancer was in her breasts. She was a relentless fighter, and I admired her strength more than anything.

I admired her strength more than anything.

In December of that year, just a few months after I'd started college, she grew more tired all of a sudden. I knew something was up. The cancer was back. And this time it wasn't breast cancer. It was leukemia. I think at the time the percentages were horrible. Something like only three percent of breast cancer survivors get leukemia. It was really bad. My dad did the same group meeting with us kids, telling all of us we were going to fight this. We were going to get through it, come hell or high water.

"We're going to do this again," he said.

Ultimately, I didn't realize how serious my mom's illness was. But it was really, really bad. I knew she was capable of beating cancer because she had done it before, but there was no preparing myself or my family for what the leukemia would do to her.

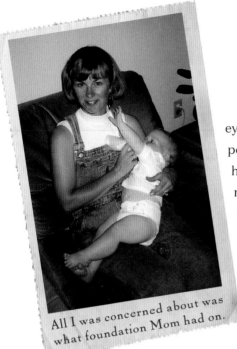

All I was concerned about was what foundation Mom had on.

It was devastating to see her dying in front of my eyes. She wasn't my mom anymore. She was a shell of a person. The chemo was harsher this time around. She had a permanent port they put in her chest for chemotherapy and radiation. All I could think was *Holy shit, this is intense.* It was like something I had seen in a movie. A "port" that gives access to the insides of your body that sits permanently on your chest? I wasn't ready to see her like that.

With her breast cancer, she had lost her hair, but she was still the same person. This time, she was fading . . . fading . . . fading. For days at a time, she would never leave bed. She had absolutely no energy.

I was no longer attending school, so I could be there for her. After she got her chemo and radiation, she would get shots. All of her cells were hitting rock bottom. She was losing an extreme amount of weight.

By March 2011, we found out that the cancer had also spread to her brain. That's when things just stopped. She was living at the hospital. But then she came home. It had gotten to a point when the doctors at the hospital literally couldn't do anything. And my mom was just like, "Fuck it, I'm not doing chemo anymore. This is too much. I need my family."

Every week she would build back up. It was like having her back for a short while, but in slow motion, because she was on a lot of pills. She would be on the phone and forget who she was speaking to. I saw this happening, but I didn't let it sink in. I had decided she was going to beat it. There was no way that wasn't going to happen. This was just temporary, and we'd get her back soon.

I rarely ever saw her cry. She was so strong for us. She believed in this concept of "Why waste time on sad things when you can make good memories?" You know? She lived life to the fullest. And, honestly, during that period, we would just hang out. We'd spend tons of time together.

It was then that she told me that when she was pregnant with me, she was sure I would be a girl. They were going to call me Lauren. And we used to talk about boys. She met this guy I was seeing. That didn't last, but I was really grateful that she was able to embrace that part of my life.

My mom and I also talked about how I wanted to move to Los Angeles. I feel she had a small window into my future. Not nearly enough, but a window.

At home, after stopping treatment, she acted more like herself. There were slow moments, but I remember saying, "She doesn't even look sick today." She was driving herself to her own checkups.

But then one day, around the end of that year or early the next, the doctors said she had only two months to live. I didn't think it was real. My brothers all cried. I didn't grieve. There was no way I was losing her. Not my mom.

The doctors moved my mom back into the hospital. My dad would wake up first thing in the morning and go to see her, would sometimes even sleep there. Adam would come home from college with Tiffany every weekend. So we would all be in the family house that didn't feel like one at all without Mom there. I got really close with Tiffany and my brothers. It was a bonding time for all of us.

And one morning, a week and a half after the doctor told us that she was going to die, we woke up, just like any other day, and made our way downtown to the hospital to see her. It was a gloomy day. It was a cold February *Twilight Zone* kind of day. We arrived at the hospital, and as the elevator doors opened, I saw all of my family members. They were all huddled outside a door.

My dad turned around and his eyes were . . . I don't know what they were, but I knew something was really bad.

"Why is everyone here?" I asked. "This is so crazy."

"She's waiting for you guys inside the room," my dad said. "We have no more time with her."

Cory, Adam, and I went in to see her, and she was just lying there. Completely still. She looked awful. She was blue in the face, hooked up to all these machines making beeping noises. I remember every time she breathed, her teeth would click slowly and quietly. She was so thin. She was probably eighty-five pounds, with no hair. It was just awful to see her like that.

Adam was bawling his eyes out. My dad was crying, too. The nurse walked out of the room to give us a moment of privacy.

"Be who you are

and say what you feel because those who mind don't matter and those who matter don't mind."

I eventually accepted the fact that she wasn't going to talk to me. But I talk to her. It's almost like praying before bed. If ever I'm feeling nervous about something or anxious or scared or happy or thankful or I wish she was there with me to see what I'm doing, I talk to her.

Once I moved to Los Angeles and I started dating Cory, my first boyfriend, I released to him a lot of the energy I'd kept bottled up inside about my mom's death. I would talk to him about it. I cried a lot about it. It made me so sad to think she would never have the chance to meet him. My mom never saw me really date someone I liked. My mom never got to meet anyone I chose to love.

Fuck, there are so many moments in my life—achievements; huge milestones; meeting Lady Gaga, for the love of God—when I feel sad she can't be there to share them with me. But I'm finally dealing with her death. I know she's here for me. She does know me as Gigi. I know she knows who I am. I know she knows that I've transitioned and where I am now. I've come to terms with it.

I wish more than anything that I could look her in the eyes and tell her this directly, of course. When she was dying, I knew that I was transgender, but I couldn't talk about it. I wish I hadn't waited to become myself. My mom would've been able to meet the real me.

My favorite photo of my mom.

My mom was so young when she died. She was forty-nine. I think she assumed I was going to be a makeup artist. I did her makeup every once in a while. But even though I had trouble with the whole college thing, I think she knew I was destined for greatness. Whenever we were out and about, we'd drive by a car dealership and I'd talk about the expensive cars I wanted to drive. Or I'd mention that she should totes incorporate some Gucci or Prada into her wardrobe (because I secretly wanted to wear it myself).

"You better get a good job when you grow up if you're going to pay for all of that," she often told me.

"Oh, bitch, I will, you just trust and believe," I said. Or something like that. It's funny to think I called my mom "bitch." But I did it in a playful way. I think we would be best friends if she were still here today.

But in all seriousness, I learned how to be a woman from my mom. I learned how to act in social situations. How to be a friend. I learned how to be a really good mom in the future. I learned my sense of humor. She was all sense of humor. She could laugh at sarcastic things, serious things, inappropriate things, all of it. She could laugh at anything and everything. Her laugh was one of her most distinct characteristics.

> I LEARNED HOW TO BE A WOMAN
> FROM MY MOM. I LEARNED
> HOW TO . . . BE A FRIEND.

I look back at pictures of her and I feel like I'm honestly her twin. I look like her. There's an energy in the photos we share. We're both definitely strong, independent, very loyal, honest, and funny women. She didn't take herself too seriously, which I always admired. She always made fun of herself. Just like I do.

My mom also used to do pageants when she was younger, with her best friend Beth, in eastern Canada. She made the move to the big city from her small town. Her big move was to Toronto, like my big move was to Los Angeles. And honestly, sometimes when I do appearances, I feel like her doing pageants. A showgirl. And my relationship with my fiancé, Nats, is a lot like my dad's with my mom. They weren't opposites that attracted, they were opposites that complemented each other perfectly. My mom was always charming and made jokes at inappropriate times. My dad was the serious one. It reminds me so much of my relationship now.

If she were around, I can't even imagine what a stage mom she would be for the life that I have. It makes me giggle. She would be so proud. I miss her every day, and if I were able to tell her one thing, I'd simply say: Thank you so much for being the world's best mom to me. There are no words to describe how much I miss you and how much I love you.

6

LIKE A BOSS

get into it or get lost

Gigi wears a Toga suit, Borsalino hat, Too Faced Born This Way Foundation, MAC Studio Fix Powder, MAC Fix Plus, Becca Tigerlily Luminous Blush, Givenchy Phenomen'Eyes Mascara, Kiehl's Lip Balm #1

I don't really remember a time before the Internet, but I definitely do remember a time before YouTube. I was in high school, and on MySpace I was Gregory Graves. Looking back, I feel like when I was Gregory Graves, *him,* I was pretending to be someone I wasn't.

I think deep down I knew the truth—that I was a trans girl—but I faked an identity, and the Internet allowed me to do that, to be someone else. At the time, Marc—"Marc with a c like Chanel," he would always say—told me to look up this girl named Michelle Phan. She did these transformation videos online with makeup. She'd transform herself into Drake, for instance.

YouTube was nothing at the time, but Marc was such a pusher that I did whatever he told me to do—with some convincing, of course. He was basically running my YouTube. He's a Virgo, and like other Virgos, he would push me to do things and it would work. That's how I know I like Virgos. They complement me really well. Along with Scorpios, Sagittarians, Cancers, and Leos. I'm sure that's totally not what the mathematically professional compatibility charts would say, but it works for me, okay?

I started making these videos called "Welcome to My Life." They were like little snippets that I would film throughout the day. I wouldn't necessarily be me. I would be more of an "extra" version of me. The Gregory Gorgeous version of me. I would try to act cooler than I was. You could do that on that Internet.

Sometimes I'd do videos with my shirt off, and I would take on this kind of macho persona. I'd talk about fucking my friends who I hadn't really had sex with. It was just to be crazy, just to be funny. I wasn't trying to make anyone *believe* it. I liked being able to say whatever I wanted to say. The people who would leave mean comments could feel safe to do it, and I could feel safe to rip them a new one in return. When I couldn't post YouTube videos, it actually made me feel alone.

I totally feel like YouTube was my diary and my therapist. I look at videos I made now and think, *How did I say and do that?* This may shock you, but I was kind of an introvert. A lot of digital influencers start that way. At the end of the day, it's you talking to your camera, alone in a bedroom. And there I was talking about sexual identity and my orientation. But YouTube was my safe space. And saying that is almost ironic, because it was being seen by hundreds of thousands of people. But I was alone filming and uploading it, so it was safe for me.

When I was being truthful, though, the videos gave people an inkling about my life, aka Gregory Gorgeous's life. Including my hair and makeup routine. And then it started with a twenty-questions tag or a fifty-questions tag. I'd let people in a little bit more. And then more and more and more and more, until I finally told my "Gay Coming-Out Story."

Talking about my life on YouTube also gave me a sense of leadership. It made me feel important and wanted. I was the only person in my province in Canada who was a YouTuber, at least that I knew. My friends in school thought it was cool. And that, in turn, made me more well-regarded and accepted. I can't even imagine how many people in high school were watching. And judging.

My mom found out that I was doing YouTube from my aunt. My cousin's best friend told my cousin. Then my cousin told my aunt, who told my mom. She said, "I know what you're doing in your room. Be careful. Don't show the inside of our house. People are crazy, you don't know what they'll do. But I love it."

I asked her if my dad knew. She told me he wasn't going to watch the videos I posted, but that yes, he did know about them. My feelings about that were complicated. I kept everything secret because I was embarrassed. It was not a *thing* like it is now. I felt kind of weird that I was doing it. There was a little shame attached. It's a lot more normal now. But it kinda hurt my feelings that my dad didn't want to watch my videos. Not that I expected him to or anything. At the same time, I didn't think he would *get* it anyway.

I never thought that starting on YouTube would end up being a job.

The truth is, I wasn't so good at working for other people. When I was starting out on YouTube—maybe I just had about a thousand followers or something at the time—I was working at McDonald's with a few of my high school girlfriends. I probably worked there for about six months. I wore a boy's uniform, but I had makeup on. I was cute.

WHEN I COULDN'T POST YOUTUBE VIDEOS, IT ACTUALLY MADE ME FEEL ALONE.

The kitchen would get hot, but I didn't hate it in there. The cinnamon buns were really good cold, when the icing hadn't melted. (They have them in Canada.) I would eat six of them at a time while hiding in the huge fridge. I probably owe like $1,000 for the cinnamon buns that I ate. They owe me, though, too. Working in fast food isn't easy!

It was more fun hanging out with my friends than trying to do well at my job. When I tried, I was good, but I was awful when I didn't. I just didn't care. I actually got written up one time because I was an awful employee. One day, I worked breakfast. I had to carry this big box of eggs. I wasn't wearing my non-slip shoes that they made me buy when I got the job. You can imagine what happened next. The whole box fell. Probably two hundred eggs, and it just oozed out the side. I messed up about 734 other things that morning, too. That was the end of that job. Written up. All in all, though, I think working at a restaurant taught me a lot about work ethic. It's very structured, and you have to follow a lot of rules. I would totes recommend it to parents who want to discipline their kids.

Then I worked at a clothing store called Bluenotes at a mall in Toronto. I bonded with Ivana, the manager of the store. She was an artist. At that time,

When I was growing up, I wanted to be an actress or a reality-television star. Some days I wanted to be in the movies, and some days I wanted to be a talk show host. My mom was obsessed with Ellen DeGeneres, Dr. Phil, and Oprah. She watched them literally every day after I got home from school. I was fascinated with their jobs, this idea of getting to know your guests and asking them anything and everything. I still think I'd be an amazing talk show host.

Regardless, I can't imagine it was easy for my parents that this was the list of possible careers I'd offered up to them. Still, I knew I'd end up in front of the camera in some form or another. Without YouTube, I don't know what I would have fallen back on. This is a dream job—just going and meeting people and being able to do what I love and inspire people and have fun while doing it.

I love it. It feels right. And I do believe that everything happens for a reason. And it's taken me to places I never, ever in a million years thought I'd get to go.

There are lots of things that I never thought I'd get to do. I never thought I'd win a Shorty Award, which honors the best in social media. I never thought I'd get to present at the MTV Video Music Awards. Or be a host on *Total Request Live*. That's so crazy. I was obsessed with Canadian VJs. They were huge celebrities in Canada. And I'm not a VJ in Canada, I'm a VJ in *America*. It's not a joke, it's not a drill. I lit up Pride events in Venice, California. That will go down in history. I've partnered with campaigns as their first transgender spokesperson. That's like "Pinch me, is this real?" shit.

And then there was my documentary. *This Is Everything: Gigi Gorgeous*. I never in a million years thought that anyone would be interested in making a documentary about me.

During my transition, I was already documenting my journey on my own. I hadn't uploaded any of it to YouTube. I would basically hoard footage. I kept it in my computer, and it was just raw stuff. Raw footage. Moments of me in my bedroom, for instance. Intimate things that I didn't automatically think made sense as a one-off video, so I never uploaded them.

I knew that I had this treasure trove, this archive of stuff, and I talked to my people about doing a movie. YouTube Red had just come out, and that was kind of like a Netflix for top YouTube creators. They were giving out deals—like maybe three a year, which wasn't really a lot at this point—and you could pitch them an idea and they would give you the money to make that idea into a legitimate project.

I suggested to my managers that we might as well pitch them a movie. YouTube said yes. We decided that I could choose my own director, which was really special, something they'd never allowed talent to do before. *So major.*

I NEVER IN A MILLION YEARS THOUGHT THAT ANYONE WOULD BE INTERESTED IN MAKING A DOCUMENTARY ABOUT ME.

I knew that I wanted a woman to tell my story. I thought that was important. I met with Barbara Kopple, who's a legendary documentarian. She's made a lot of movies, but I'd already watched *Shut Up and Sing,* which is about the Dixie Chicks. We sat down and we connected. We vibed. She was really unfiltered, and I loved that. That's like me. I knew she would have only one chance to get to the bottom of my story. But I knew that she would get to the bottom of it.

I had to give up total control, though, which was different for me. I always have control over what I edit and post, and I had all this footage. I thought I would be able to edit it myself. I asked if it was okay, but YouTube Red and Barbara Kopple said no. That, for sure, was nerve-racking, but the documentary was fun. I was trying something new. If they'd let me, I would change some things about the movie—namely, that I would put a little bit more in it about my friends and my current relationship—but I thought it was really, really good. (And so, btw, did *The New York Times.*)

It's crazy how many places I've gotten to go because the documentary was so successful. And it made me want to do more things. Like write this book.

And so I'm not done yet. Though it's not what the title means, the truth is that I want to do everything. There are so many things to do. And the sky's the limit.

I want to build an empire. I want to have a fragrance. I want to have a clothing line. Ultimately, I want to be a voice for the LGBTQ movement. I want to show kids everywhere that your dreams are achievable. I want to be in a movie, for sure. I've always wanted to be in an action movie: Megan Fox in *Transformers*, a Bond Girl, or Wonder Woman. I think that would be so sick. I love badass girls in movies. It would be big for me, but also for trans girls everywhere.

I want to make a mark in this world. I want the stuff I stand for to live past the years I have on this planet. To be a legend. An icon.

In the short term, it would mean that I'd get a Madame Tussauds statue of me, posing for the red carpet, in my million-dollar dress that August Getty made. That dress is the one that's totally going to be it. I actually just came up with that idea now. That's a new goal. A Bobblehead would also be cute. There must be a way that you can personalize and order those things on the Internet. Nats: Are you reading this? You're probably not reading this. Shit.

I want to make a mark in this world. I want the stuff I stand for to live past the years I have on this planet. To be a legend. An icon.

THE SUBTLE ART OF

BEING "EXTRA"

Being "extra" is just something you don't see every day. It's about having fun with your style, personality, environment, and any situation you find yourself in. It's about not taking yourself too seriously, about taking things to the extreme, thinking outside of the box, *the next level.* Being extra is a lot more fun than just being regular. Why wear a little black dress when you can wear a sequined rainbow gown?

When I'm full glam, for sure I love the attention. If you're going to go to an event and you're getting all dressed up and getting your picture taken, you might as well go all the way. My friends call me a monster sometimes. I love it. That's how my style has evolved, though. I used to be extra all the time. Now I know there's a time and a place. I've totally embraced my casual, laid-back side.

Part of being extra is that you know what you're doing is ridiculous. You're kind of in on the joke. It's about not taking it *too* seriously. If you have a pink shoe, add a pink lipstick, a pink bag, a pink nail, a pink wig. It's just about being stupid. But in a way, that's kind of everything, right? Are you picking up what I'm putting down?

One of the fun things about being extra is that anyone can be extra. Extra is a lifestyle. It's definitely for pictures and moments. And the pictures get you attention. Being extra looks good in pictures because it's basically dressing for a photo shoot. It's so not practical, but it's also so good. It's like being a real live dress-up doll sometimes, like a Barbie. It's the best. At least to me it is.

I've learned over the years, especially since my mom died, that if you take yourself too seriously, life just isn't that fun. I've always been able to laugh at myself. This way, you're in control of the joke, so nobody can make fun of you.

There are a few times when being extra isn't the best idea, including:

♦

WHEN YOU WAKE UP HUNGOVER.

That's probably because it takes lots of extra effort
to be extra, and when you're hungover, it's just
really hard to make that effort. But then again, you
could totally do the most with a look or vibe when
you're hungover. For example, look the WORST
you possibly can, go out in public, and stumble
everywhere. That would be hilarious.

♦

WHEN THE LAW'S INVOLVED.

You don't want to get in trouble with the law just
because you've been a little extra, you know? Unless
it's just a warning or something. Then you can.

That said, sometimes it's too much being Gigi. When my schedule's very
full, going to the club can be too much. If one person recognizes you, you know
that they're watching, so you can't act a fool. You can't be yourself. You definitely have to show up sober to be extra.

The most extra I've ever been was when I went skydiving and started
Vogueing in mid-air. People skydiving are usually scared for their lives. I was
worried that I was getting the Vogueing right as I flew the sky.

I know this is getting a little un-Gigi, but the thought of everyone being
extra gives me hope for the world. All of this hardship and war and just plain
old crap? Wearing a gorgeous, funny outfit and acting silly in it honestly makes
my life a better one. And I think it'll help yours, too.

7

PLANES, TRANS,

AND

AUTOMOBILES

one-way ticket to the real me

Gigi wears a Burberry trench, Jeffree Star Androgyny Eyeshadow Palette, Make Up For Ever Lip Liner, MAC Myth Satin Lipstick, Lilly Lashes Miami

and whomever was handling it flew me down from Toronto for it and paid me turnt money. I probably agreed to do a YouTube video for them. But it meant a free trip to NYC, and I lo-o-o-ve the city.

They flew me out for four days. Four days in New York! It was bananas. And I had to work for only one day, and work involved going to a fashion show. I mean, really? It didn't seem like work at the time. My manager, Scott, had also arranged in this deal that I had to "recover" from the travel, so I needed extra days with a paid hotel in New York City. Perfection!

I mean, Toronto is like an hour-long flight to New York. You don't need to recover from that. It was the most ridiculous thing to me, but it was also amazing. To this day I sort of can't believe this is what my life was becoming.

And the fashion show was a crazy thing. It was just a real *moment* for me. I didn't know what to expect from the event and from New York Fashion Week, since it was my first one, but I didn't have to do really anything except take pictures and tag *Just Dance*. I got to sit in the front row. We went backstage. It was just lights, camera, action to be in New York for Fashion Week. I kind of felt like I wasn't deserving, that I wasn't worthy. That I was scamming the system in some way to be at the event with all these important people.

I still feel like that a lot of the time when I'm out and about. I love it. I hope it never goes away.

I saw Kendall Jenner walk for the first time at the show. Kris Jenner and Kylie were in the audience, too. I had watched them on their E! show *Keeping Up with the Kardashians*. I just looked at them, thinking, *They're so famous, they're so major, this is crazy*. And wow, they support Kendall a lot.

Yasmine Petty, who was a well-known model at the time, walked in the show, too. Her boobs were so freaking huge. Her proportions were so exaggerated. Her curvaceous body and stunning face owned the runway. When I saw her, the crowd erupted with whispering. I knew she was controversial for her look, but what were they

Meeting Amanda Lepore and David LaChappelle.

whispering about? And given her over-the-top look, all I could think was: *How did she scam* her *way here?*

My friend clued me in to the reason for all the whispers: Yasmine was a friend of hers, and she was transgender. I saw Yasmine after the show. She acted as if we were best friends the second I met her. That same day, my friend showed me a picture he said was a picture of her naked, which included what he said was her huge dick. It was crazy. She was so gorgeous and feminine, and then to think that she had such a big dick was a little bit of a mind fuck. I was mesmerized by her beauty. Honestly, I felt a little scared of her and I felt a little like Alice in Wonderland, in this place where nothing was what it seemed. But I also felt that in New York, anything and everything was possible.

And it was. It was a place where I really was around trans people for the first time. They weren't like people I'd seen on television. They were in fashion. They were at clubs. They were living these big lives. And they started realizing who I was.

The night after the *Just Dance* fashion show, my friend Kyle invited me out. He's an androgynous model who has a kind of crazy, out-there look. I'd met him in Toronto. He's a nightlife personality. To this day, I see him when I go to New York or he comes to L.A. or Toronto. He's so fun and so real.

Anyway, the second night I was in Manhattan, he invited me over to Amanda Lepore's apartment. And I almost shit a brick.

Amanda Lepore is this living legend. An icon. She's not human. She's so out-of-this-world beautiful. Well, *I* think she's stunning. I remember I brought a bottle of Belvedere vodka to Amanda's house. I don't even know how I *bought* the bottle of vodka, given that I was underage.

Her apartment is this tiny, tiny room. Probably smaller than a rug you have at home, especially if you live somewhere where real estate is fucked. And here, I'm using the word *fucked* to mean cheap. Because it's definitely not cheap in New York Fucking City.

In Amanda's apartment, Louboutin shoeboxes made up an entire wall. There were probably two hundred of them. All labeled with pictures. There was a bed with a cheetah-print duvet cover. There was a sink, but no bathroom.

At Amanda's apartment, grocery store ready.

I heard once that Amanda pays only $500 a month. Five hundred dollars, I learned, is really nothing for rent in New York. She's lived there for like forty years or something. Like I said, living legend.

After I gave her the vodka and we hung with her shoeboxes for a little bit, we went out. We went to the Boom Boom Room, which is this club at the top of the Standard Hotel overlooking the West Side Highway. And everyone was taking pictures. Kyle and Amanda knew *everyone,* and I didn't know anybody.

That's where I saw "Betty" for the first time.

Betty was going to play a huge part in my transition and the woman I was going to become in the very, *very* near future. We casually said hi and I didn't really think about her twice. But we ended up staying at the Boom Boom Room until about three or four in the morning, and then we went to Cafeteria restaurant afterward for food and more drinks. That's this place on Seventeenth Street and Seventh Avenue in Chelsea that's open twenty-four hours. Used to be one of my favorite spots to go when I was in town.

It turns out all the club kids gather there to get food before the sun rises. I was learning so much already!

We were just chilling, but once I saw Betty in the light I noticed something different about her. Something special. A star quality. An extreme beauty to her face and demeanor. I just kept thinking, *She's so freaking gorgeous.* I loved the shape of her face. She was feminine and soft-looking. Like a doll.

Before I knew it, she scooched right next to me. "You're beautiful," she told me. I was wearing this little mini red completely see-through lace dress from American Apparel (OMG, what was I thinking?). I was basically naked at this point. I was actually trying for the whole "Amanda Lepore look." It was extremely flattering for a woman as beautiful as Betty to tell me I looked good. And she had me interested.

Well, we started talking and she started asking me about my identity. It turned out she was transgender. She told me what she'd had done to her face.

She had gotten her forehead shaved down, and a nose job as well. She had her lips and cheeks done, and her jaw and her chin. I remember thinking she looked so natural, how could this be?

Before I met Betty, I had only seen plastic surgery that looked really fake, that looked over-the-top. You know, like Amanda Lepore's (I worship her, but it's true), or things I'd seen on television. When Betty told me she'd had all these things done to herself, I didn't believe her. I thought she looked amazing and completely natural.

"Are you fucking kidding me?" I asked her.

She was like, "Yeah, have you ever thought about doing this yourself? You'd be even more beautiful and feminine."

She was referring to the things she'd done to change her body.

And I said, "Oh my God, that's so crazy."

Up to that point I hadn't ever thought about surgery. But I was fascinated with vanity, that's for sure. It was completely educational talking with her. As far as I was concerned, we were the only people in the room once we started talking. Everyone else just disappeared. I wanted to know where she went to get everything she had done. I wanted to know everything about her.

> ## SHE WAS LIKE, "YEAH, HAVE YOU EVER THOUGHT ABOUT DOING THIS YOURSELF? YOU'D BE EVEN MORE BEAUTIFUL AND FEMININE."

If being trans was a drug, she was a pusher for sure. She insisted I wasn't gay. That it wasn't the right label for me, if we believe that labels even exist.

"No, you're not gay," she said. "You're trans, you fit in here. You're a woman."

Of course I wanted Betty to keep talking. So she did. "I'm looking in a mirror five years ago," she told me.

She fully made me realize the truth about myself. And it was almost the exact same conversation I'd have a few years later, but from the other side of the transition, with a few of my trans sisters. Betty was speaking from her heart,

Scott and me back in the day.

being a genuine trans girl helping another trans girl, just one who didn't know she was.

I asked her to drive me home to my hotel. In the taxi, on the way, she took off her top and showed me her boobs. Her boobs were HUMONGOUS. It was super-fun meeting a new girlfriend and talking all night, but the sun was coming up and I had a flight to catch in the morning. That night was a complete revelation for me.

It's hard to remember what happened after that. It was such a major turning point of an evening. I went back up to the tiny hotel room I was sharing with Scott for the trip. It was on the Lower East Side, and the hotel was under construction, so walking past the workers at eight a.m. in my skimpy club dress was anything but comfortable. It was more than kind of a mess. I got back into the room and I woke him up and said, "Oh my God, I met this girl tonight." And I told him all about Betty and that I really wanted to be like her.

I knew that I wanted to do exactly what she had done.

He saw how excited I was, but he said, "Okay, Greg. Take it easy. Take it slow." And I said, "No, I want to do this now." A lot of the time, Scott will roll his eyes and be like, "Oh, Gigi." I don't think he knew how serious I was. But I was completely serious. I'd never been more serious about anything in my life.

I went to bed (or more of a nap, because we had to be at the airport in a few hours) realizing that I was transgender. Seeing myself fully for the first time. I was going to do this for myself. I was going to do the things other trans girls had done. And I wanted to start immediately.

I wasn't sad at all. I wasn't wistful. I didn't think twice about it. I was over the moon. I had the money, so I didn't need to worry about that. And I had all the means to do this. I think the only thing I was even remotely nervous about was what my dad would think and what my brothers would say. But I knew that that was the next step. I had never been more certain of anything.

Betty is what I call my "trans mom" in the community. She was very important in helping me to decide who I was and exactly how I wanted to achieve it. She really guided me. Everyone needs that person for things that are far smaller in life than transitioning. Even if I always felt the person she was guiding me toward was *exactly me,* it's still an intense process.

It really helps to have someone who's been through it all to kind of show you the way. To tell you about hormones and how they work, to talk you through where to get your surgery, to be your emotional support. Your rock.

Your family and friends can rally around you, but they really can't answer questions specific to the trans experience in the same way someone who has gone through it can. Questions like: "What kind of hormones do I need?" "What exactly is FFS?" (It's facial feminization surgery.) "What about dating?"

Like a great wise person once said: Fake it until you make it.

Betty was the person who was motherly to me (not long after I lost my mother, actually). She was also a teacher. With Betty, it was always "class is in session."

She was an important guide to me, though she certainly was a character. We would text a lot, and she came to stay with me in Canada in the winter while I was on hormones. I remember her getting off the plane when it was freezing out. Twenty degrees! But she didn't act as if it was freezing cold. She had on a sundress and sandals and was carrying a huge Louis Vuitton duffel bag. I was waiting for her at the airport. Everyone had on parkas and jeans and boots and I was like, "Who does this bitch think she is? It's CANADA, girl!"

Theoretically, Betty came from New York, but it was as if she stepped out of a fantasy. She wore Giuseppe Zanotti sandals the whole time, even when it was snowing out. I remember seeing her feet while she was wearing them. Her feet were blue. They were covered in snow! So, yes, she was more than a character. I knew she was out to lunch, but I loved it.

But even though she was unique and totally crazy, in a lot of ways she was the most helpful person in my life when it came to finding myself. I was nervous to tell my friends that I was transitioning, but she convinced me to talk to them. She told me it's never as bad as you think it's going to be, and she was right. (Good advice for you to remember, too.)

Breaking the news wasn't as bad as I'd feared, but that doesn't mean it was easy. My friends were gagging. They were skeptical. It was hard for them to wrap their heads around it. Marc, for instance, always reminded me that I'd told him I never wanted to be a girl.

After I told my friends, I told my family. I started with my brothers, which I thought would be a gateway to my dad. I told Cory, my younger brother, first. I'm a lot more impulsive than he is, but he tends to trust my intuition. He didn't have much to say, but he did have questions. He asked if taking hormones was safe. He wanted to know what to call me, if it meant I was going to have surgery.

Adam, my older brother, came next. It was a little bit harder to talk to him because I hadn't been living with him for the last two years like I had been with Cory. He had the same questions as Cory. He seemed scared of the changes that would happen, especially when it came to plastic surgery. Neither of them wanted me to go under the knife. They didn't want me mutilating my body. I didn't talk to my dad until a few months after that.

It didn't hurt my feelings that my friends and family couldn't completely understand what I was going through. It was hard for me to imagine them fully understanding me at that time anyway. But Betty could.

Still, I don't know a lot about Betty. Today, we're not in touch, so I can't ask her where she came from, or what she saw in me back then. For instance, I don't even know what Betty really did for a living. She told me she was a burlesque dancer, but I've never seen her perform. She wanted to be Dita Von Teese very badly. I would question her, but she would always find a way to divert my questions and not give me straight answers. So I ended up dropping it out of respect for her privacy.

She ended up lying to me about a lot of stuff. And I don't even know why. And then she did something that really broke my trust. She came to visit me in Los

Angeles, and I confided in her about Scott, my manager. I was having a moment where I'd stopped seeing him as one of my best friends; I saw him as more of a business partner (which he of course also was). Without telling me, she went ahead and met him for lunch and repeated our whole conversation to him word for word. She made how I felt seem bad. I'd been trying to work out my feelings with her. She turned around and twisted and manipulated the entire situation.

"Why would you do that? Why would you try to ruin our relationship?" I asked her. I think she had two goals: She was sabotaging the relationship I had with Scott, and she was also trying to sabotage the relationship she and I had. We haven't spoken since.

She may have been trying to sabotage our relationship because I was starting to find a new life in Los Angeles, where I met more people who saw me with fresh eyes. Maybe I didn't need her as much anymore. Maybe she sensed that. I'll never know for sure. All I know is once trust is broken in any relationship, it's very hard to get it back. Even if you're sisters.

Betty may not always have had my best interests at heart. Okay, if I'm telling the real truth, I think she's a super-manipulative person. But as everything "trans" goes, she really opened up the world to me. It would have taken me a helluva lot longer if Betty hadn't shown me the way. Even when we weren't friends, she did want the best for me in that sense. She can relate. And when you're trans, sometimes it's hard to find people who can.

INSECURITY:

THE OPPOSITE OF

"EXTRA"

Being a little bit "extra" sometimes is also a pretty decent way to cover up when you feel insecure or you're feeling a little bit of social anxiety coming on. Do I feel those things ever? you may ask. And I will answer the only way I know how. Hundo P. I feel insecure all the time.

For instance, sometimes I feel it when I wake up and I don't feel as if I look good, or I feel like I look fat or like a man (again, ugh). Sometimes I feel it when people are looking at my hair, but I think they're staring right at my scar from my FFS on my forehead, the surgery I had on my face. My scar is a big source of insecurity for me, even though my friends tell me they can barely see it. Still, it's a complex that I have. Some days it bothers me more than others.

Sometimes I'm also insecure about my shoulders. I feel like I look really broad, which tends to be a really masculine trait. Some girls get their asses done to balance out their shoulders so they don't look so wide in comparison. That's something I've seriously considered doing but haven't got the balls to yet. Or completely decided if I want that Kim Kardashian hourglass figure. I kind of like being slim-hipped most of the time.

Also, my hands. Sometimes I think my hands are really big and veiny and manly and/or chubby and sausagelike. That's why I'm rarely ever seen without acrylic tips on. They give my fingers extension. I feel like they instantly make them more feminine. And it's also easier to style my hair with them. They're like built-in combs.

A *lot* of trans girls are super-insecure about their feet. I think my feet are just fine, however. I actually really, really like them. I got lucky with the size of them, I can fit into designer shoes no problem, and stores almost always have my size in stock.

But see: You kind of can't really win. There will always be parts of your body that bother you. You can fix them with surgery, maybe. But even if you find a way to control the things you don't like, you will probably just turn around and find something else to be insecure about. Once one "problem" is gone, you search for another one.

No doubt, it helps to have people around you who are rooting for you, who have your best interests at heart. And I seriously feel as if I have that. A lot of my friends and basically all of my family hate that I pick my face and body apart. I think that's important to have around you. If I was surrounded with people pushing me to get every surgery I've ever said I wanted to get, I would look like that cat lady Jocelyn Wildenstein at this point. Google Images her. *Hundo P.*

The truth is, you're probably thinking about your insecurities more than anyone is actually thinking about you. Confidence is one of the sexiest things you can have. And like a great wise person once said: Fake it until you make it.

I do think makeup can make you feel a lot better about yourself. It can help you do things you wouldn't normally do. I learned that a lot through surgery. I got really depressed after I did my face. It almost stripped me of my confidence. It made me feel like a monster. And not the good kind of monster, but a hideous creature. Like Frankenstein's monster. I thought the second I would wake up from my FFS I'd be extremely confident. It was literally the other way around.

I'm not saying it's easy to ignore those feelings, but I had to figure out a way to. And whether that's through makeup or your friends or just Mary Poppins-y spoonfuls of emotional sugar, you've got to keep on keepin' on. See, I just became Bob Dylan there.

The truth is, you're
probably thinking
about your insecurities
more than anyone
is actually thinking
about you.

8

---- ♦ ----

NEW LIPS,
BREASTS,
AND
CRYING

FOR THE FIRST TIME EVER

---- ♦ ----

welcome to
womanhood

Gigi wears It Cosmetics
CC Cream, Givenchy
Phenomen'Eyes Mascara,
Kiehl's Lip Balm #1, Hourglass
Ambient Lighting Powder,
Morphe Continuous Setting Mist

When I met Betty, she told me that the first thing I needed to do in order to start my transition was to get on HRT (hormone replacement therapy).

To do so, I needed to go to an endocrinologist. So I found out what endocrinology exactly was. Google it, like I did, if you need to. It's the study of hormones. So I needed a hormone doctor. And I found one in my area of Toronto, who, as it turned out, typically helped old people going through menopause. Google menopause, too, if you need to. I'm not going to explain everything!

I went to the doctor alone. I didn't tell anyone what I was doing—not my brothers, not my dad, not my friends. I drove my ass to the building. I got to the office and started filling out all the paperwork in the waiting room. I was the youngest person there by far. I guess people could guess that the teenage boy wasn't going through menopause. I felt super-awkward. Now I'm totally and completely used to "awkward," but I'm more used to awkward *now* than I was used to awkward *then*.

One of the questions on the paperwork was "Why are you here?" And Carrie Bradshaw–style, I couldn't help but wonder: Why *am* I here? Do I write that I'm here because I want to transition into a woman? That I want hormones? Do I write I don't really know what else to do? Do I write "Because Betty told me I needed to find an endocrinologist and I looked you up online"? I had no idea what to write.

I must have written something, because the doctor eventually called me in to his office with a shocked expression on his face. I was a different kind of case than the women he usually saw. Maybe he thought I was fifty like all his other patients, but just had a really turnt surgeon that made me look really young. I don't know.

He was an older doctor. He sat me down. It was one on one. And you know how intense that can be. He asked why I was there. I said, "I want to be a woman, and I want to take the steps to do so."

He replied, "How sure are you?"

I rolled back a little bit. I didn't want to be too forward, but I still wanted to convey that I was sure. I told him, "I'm not looking for a sex change, I'm just looking for hormones." (I probably wouldn't use the term *sex change* now, by the way. It's gender reassignment surgery. More on that later.)

He was very nice and understanding. He told me that in order to get hormones, he thought I needed a note from a therapist who had analyzed me. He gave me his cell phone number and said, "Whenever you get in touch with this therapist, we can get this sorted out." I should have been happy. I should have been in a good mood. This was moving along. I was on the right track, making progress. But when I walked out of that office, I felt devastated.

I went to my car, and I cried my eyes out. I thought that the transition was never going to happen for me. That's the kind of person I am. If it doesn't happen now, if things don't happen absolutely immediately, hundo P, I get really, really upset.

After breaking down for a few minutes in the parking lot, I pulled it together. I thought of anything I could do *today* to make this whole situation better. I thought about the therapist my dad made me and my brothers go see when my mom passed away. Could she give me a note saying I could start hormones? Nah, I didn't even like her. I had to figure something out. And quick.

So I went home and I did some more Googling. I Googled "gender confusion" and "therapy" and "sex change" and a therapist in the area came up. I called her. I think she had a home practice. Again, I didn't tell anybody what I was doing, but I made an appointment that day and went over.

We talked about everything.

At first, like the endocrinologist, she was surprised at my youth. She said she hadn't dealt with someone like me in years. I was so young and so sure of myself. And maybe there weren't many transgender people in the area at the time.

I talked about wanting to be on hormones. I told her I saw my friend Betty do it and it was fine. This is what I wanted. This was the beginning step toward transitioning. I even knew the dosage of Spironolactone and Estrodiol I wanted to start myself on.

She talked me through the severity of taking hormones. She had lots of warnings that I honestly didn't want to hear. That they might irreversibly

DON'T HATE ME BECAUSE I'M SKINNY. THERE ARE PLENTY OF OTHER REASONS.

change my body. That they might cause crying fits due to hormone imbalances. That they weren't necessarily dangerous, but they might be unsafe and might make me unstable. That breast tissue would form and I would need surgery to remove the breast tissue if I ever decided to stop taking them. Also I would be rapidly gaining body fat in my hips and ass.

Basically, she tried to scare me, but it didn't work. She told me she'd seen people transition and regret it. "I don't want this for you. You're too young and beautiful already," she said.

I don't know if you can guess, but I definitely did not connect with this woman. I felt she wasn't trying to understand me at all, like she'd already made her own decision about what was right for me. It was very hard to convince her. With the endocrinologist, I felt like I could be all "Pleeeeeeasse" and flirty. But this woman gave me a tougher time. All I wanted was that note, and I acted crazy and shameless to get it. If that whole session had been recorded, it probably would be priceless. (Look, I'm used to living my life on YouTube and having a record of everything.) I kept

Everyone needs a good selfie before leaving the house.

thinking, *If this is going to be who I have to plead my case to, then so be it.*

I just said, "I want this," and I stuck to my guns. I would have come back to her again and again if I had to, but I think she saw the truth in me. She saw that I was unwavering in going after what I wanted. She sent a note via fax to the endocrinologist. I had done it! In one session, I'd gotten the note!

I still didn't know what I was doing, but I went back to his office to see the doctor. I think I was just determined to make this happen. One-track mind. I'm not one to give up on what I want—ever. And if this endocrinologist wouldn't help me, then I would try to find another endocrinologist who would.

"I heard you met with a therapist," he told me. "I think we're going to start you on this low dose of Estrogel and work up to pills."

I thought to myself, *Gel? Gel?! I want the hormone pills!* I guess we were learning together. I went with what the doctor advised.

I started on estrogen lotion that you rub on the insides of your thighs. I remember in as little as a week I saw a difference in my chest. It was crazy to me that a gel could absorb into my body so quickly and cause such a fast change. Then the doctor moved me on to a testosterone blocker called Spironolactone. Betty hadn't told me about the estrogen-lotion aspect of things, and I'd never really heard about it. But it's a way to introduce estrogen into your system slowly, so it was the correct step to take. I would put it on religiously, and I started noticing actual breasts develop. My nipples were really, really sore and puffy. But I liked the feeling. It meant things were changing.

Before I started on the hormones, I wasn't a big crier. Those tears outside the endocrinologist's office were totally out of the ordinary. I wasn't all that emotional, or even sympathetic sometimes. I cried when my mom died, but not nearly as much as my brothers did. I don't know. I'm not saying there's one correct response when it comes to grief, but I recognize that my reaction to her death—a really huge life event—was a little muted.

When I first started on the medication, I didn't feel any different. As I stayed on the hormones longer, though, it felt as if my brain was balancing out. I felt leveled. I felt normal. I was more in tune with my emotions than I had ever been before. I don't think I'd ever cried at movies before, but here, now, I finally could. And I was doing the same thing with commercials. I was welling up at commercials for kids in Africa. Commercials for dogs that have no home. I was crying at dog commercials! Thank you, God, for this miracle!

I liked crying. No, I loved it. I feel like I hadn't cried for years at a time and I was making up for it now. I had been expressing myself in other ways, like being "extra." What I liked most about crying was that it made me really feel feminine. I had always been super-jealous of my girlfriends who were more sympathetic toward people in tough situations than I was. If they were going through a hard time, I found it very hard to care. The hormones opened up some part of me that let my body feel things, things that were sad in my life and in the lives of others. It hadn't felt natural to be so stoic, and I felt better now that I had a release for the emotions that'd been bottled up inside. It was like one of the many puzzle pieces that fit together.

Because of my years as a diver, I was really, really thin and really muscular. I had little to no body fat because I was constantly active from a young age. But then came the hormones, which developed breast tissue. I didn't have a lot going on in that department—I gave myself a serious upgrade on my twenty-first birthday, which you'll hear all about—but I had a *little* bit going on.

With the hormones, I started gaining some weight, which most girls, as I see it now, would hate. But I loved it. I was always so skinny, so a few pounds didn't matter much. (Don't hate me because I'm skinny. There are plenty of other reasons.)

Hormones also started giving me puffy nipples, and a tiny bit of breast tissue around them. The nipples and that tiny bit of breast tissue were actually very sensitive. I had never felt anything there before. It didn't necessarily feel *good* sensitive. It was more of a bad sensitive. At that time, any kind of rubbing against the puffy nipples and breast tissue was unbearable. Even if I was wearing a loose shirt, if it rubbed up against them the wrong way, I would squeal in discomfort. It was actually so bad that I needed to wear a camisole under all of my clothing to hug my body. I was obsessed with camisoles. I had them in literally every single color, to go with any outfit I wore. They were kind of like my first training bra. Or I'd wear this tight Juicy velour tracksuit. It was tight as fuck.

But because I had even the beginnings of breasts . . . the *semblance* of breasts . . . *breast vibes,* if you will . . . I loved it. Things were happening. But that also meant other people were starting to notice them. Like my dad.

I was being a lazy asshole at home, and of course in casual knockabout wear, my Juicy velour tracksuit. These triangular mounds on my chest poked up. They weren't supernoticeable, but they were noticeable *enough.*

Doing what I do best! Recording YouTube videos, duh!

One day my dad asked me straight out, "Did you get your breasts injected? They're looking full." I was GAGGED he had noticed, let alone said something to me about their appearance.

I don't know why I couldn't tell him the truth. That I'd secretly found this endocrinologist and that

Doing some home repairs in the kitchen with Tiffany.

Doing dishes after family dinner with Cory. Or at least he was, LOL.

I had started taking hormones. In retrospect, it would have been the right thing to do. But I guess I couldn't do it. I couldn't have the conversation with him. I felt he wouldn't understand and would want to get involved and ruin what I had planned for myself.

Now I know that I was grieving the loss of my mom, and my dad was grieving the loss of her, too. No doubt, it would have been a good time to get closer. And I probably would have felt a lot better telling him the truth.

But I didn't.

I just said, "God, no, Dad, no. I don't even know if you *can* inject breasts."

I definitely didn't tell him that I was on hormones. I definitely didn't tell him that I was having *breast vibes.* As I moved along in making changes in my body, however, it became harder and harder not to start talking about it. The next step, for instance.

It was harder for me to hide my lips. They were front and center, literally.

Getting my lips done was my first cosmetic procedure ever. Lip injections have become very popular in recent years, but when I did them, nobody I knew had them.

I always hated my lips. My whole family has thin lips. It was more of a joke for everyone else, not something to stress about. When I would smile, my upper lip would not even exist. You've seen those thin Oreos that people eat to pre-

My lips were a whole lot frigging thinner than a thin Oreo.

tend they aren't really eating regular Oreos? My lips were a whole lot frigging thinner than a thin Oreo. Not cute.

I really wanted fuller lips. I was often wearing full-on makeup at that time, and bigger lips would give more surface area for my lipsticks and give me a sexier, more feminine look. When you do your makeup, there are only certain parts of your face that are exciting. Foundation was fun in the beginning, because I got to play with different textures, formulas, undertones, and colors. I got to pick my favorites. If your skin doesn't look good, then your whole face doesn't look good. I wanted to wear makeup, but I wanted it to seem as if I wasn't wearing makeup.

After foundation, I started to get excited about eyebrows, and I would go crazy with filling my eyebrows in. Then it was all about the lipsticks. I wanted to show off more color, and with thin lips, you have only a little slit.

Getting a lip injection was not a big deal at all. Super-casual, actually. It was kind of like getting a blowout, but more expensive. Like $600 the first time I did it. But I didn't blink at the price. Oh, no, I was spending much more than that on orders from Forever 21.

Lips were one of the easier parts of my transformation. They were achievable. They were affordable. (Okay, for me they were affordable. The total transformation I saw for myself wasn't going to come cheap.) It's a fact that getting your lips done is not an invasive procedure. For me, it was basically a nurse with a syringe going straight into my thin, thin lips. You'll hear me say this a lot: I have a high pain tolerance. Especially when it's for things to deal with vanity. But I'll tell you this: Even though it was super-easy and straightforward to get my lips injected, I was surprised to find out that it was actually really painful.

The other thing about getting lip injections is it isn't so easy to hide. It's not like you can hide your lips under a Juicy tracksuit. Why in the hell would you do that, anyway? But I couldn't selectively hide the

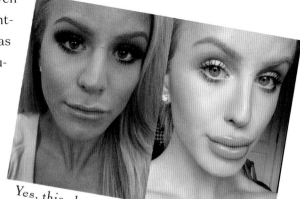

Yes, this photo was taken on the same day. And yes I regret it.

It's like the physical process, too: First you start with hormones, then you move on to lips. The next stop, at least for me, was figuring out what to do about my Adam's Apple.

lip injections from my dad, like I could the nipples under a camisole. I had to tell him, because it was noticeable. I had huge black-and-blue bruises almost instantly after the nurse had finished.

Still, at this point, I was nineteen, and I could really make my own choices and decisions. And it was my money. I'd paid for it.

Before I worked up the nerve to tell my dad what I'd done, he confronted me. I don't remember what he said exactly.

Christmas with most of my family on my dad's side

He said something like "I wish you wouldn't have done that." He didn't say a lot more than that, but I could tell on the inside he was like, *Why the hell did you do that?* He didn't understand it. At the time, I thought my dad didn't understand anything, at least when it came to what was going on with me. Now, of course, I'm on the other side of the transformation and I have a lot more compassion.

But even so, my dad's a bit conservative. He's the kind of person who, even at his age, with three grown kids, is still worried about whether his own parents will approve. He'll ask me to "dial down the look a little bit" whenever we get together with them for a family gathering. To not wear something too crazy, or to cover up more than usual. "What are Grandma and Grandpa going to think?" He's still like that, but I've learned to accept that he's like that, just like he's learned to accept that I'm the way I am.

This is all part of the emotional process. Baby steps. You start in a place of not understanding each other, then you start to understand each other a teensy little bit more than before. It's all about the various stops on the train.

It's like the physical process, too: First you start with hormones, then you move on to lips. The next stop, at least for me, was figuring out what to do about my Adam's Apple.

THE IMPORTANCE OF PRONOUNS

I know I sometimes make light of matters and I can be cheeky when talking about my life and transition, but I want to make it clear that this hasn't necessarily been an easy road. And the pathway is not just a surgical one. It's very emotional, too.

One of the harder things has been dealing with my extended family. I thought once I told them that I wanted to be called Gigi, they would refer to me as "she" and as "Gigi" and I wouldn't have to keep reiterating it to them. But apparently that wasn't the case. Whenever members of my family would slip up on the pronouns or my name, I would get very discouraged.

I was of the mindset that if someone close to you is transitioning, you do what they ask you to do. You don't slip up. It's rude. If I'd be at a family gathering or at a Christmas meal and someone would call me by my old name, Gregory, it not only felt embarrassing, it also felt like a giant "fuck you" to me and all the work I was doing on myself.

I know I'm just talking about a pronoun. At least now that I feel less emotionally entangled and tied up about it, I can refer to it as "just a pronoun." But I'm such a control freak that, at that time, it felt so discouraging. I had planned it all. I had put all this mental exertion, all this time and energy into my transition. I had told everyone behind the scenes. And for people to still slip up was incredibly discouraging.

All I could think was, *Dude, I still feel like a guy, but I'm pushing to feel like a woman.* For me to say I'm a woman is one thing. But to feel it and have people acknowledge it is another thing. I would wake up and feel great, and then someone would knock me down by calling me by the wrong pronoun or the wrong name. In the beginning, when you don't have the physical attributes, the pronouns are the only thing you have. Sometimes, they're the only real thing you can latch on to that make you feel more like your gender.

That's what I went through. But now I recognize that my previous perspective was immature and, probably, lacking in compassion. My family members had to transition, too. It's not like this had been in my family. No one in my family had ever met someone transgender before me.

The only advice I can give is if you know someone who's transitioning, give them a compliment. You don't know what they're going through, and you never know how much it means to them.

9

NEXT-LEVEL SURGERY,

OR LIKE BEING IN A

HORROR MOVIE

Gagged

Gigi wears a vintage '50s set, Too Faced Born This Way Foundation, Tarte Shape Tape Concealer, Givenchy Blonde Eyebrow Pencil, Givenchy Phenomen'Eyes Mascara, MAC Pink Swoon Blush, Becca Champagne Pop Highlighter, Colourpop White Eyeliner

Next on my list was the trachea shave. At that point, I was twenty, and I was going to Los Angeles frequently. Sometimes for brand deals and appearances, but more often because I was starting to like it there. It was far from my Toronto life. I felt that when I touched down at LAX, I was in my world. I was starting to make new friends who liked going out at night. They didn't care about my old life as a boy. They knew me as Gigi.

On a trip in the fall a few months after my mom died, I decided that I'd extend my trip and stay for a week and a half. There were parties and stuff I needed or wanted to go to, but I also needed to move on to my personal next step.

I called a plastic surgeon in Beverly Hills about shaving my trachea down so it would be smooth, not so prominent. I did my research. He did them all the time. He also said the cartilage around my throat was blocking my voice box and suggested opening that up to cut and sew back together my vocal cords, which would change my voice. I don't know if I had money for that at the time, but I was also scared I would end up mute or something crazy. The idea of having a more feminine voice was enticing, but I didn't want to not be able to speak, like the Little Mermaid. (More connections!) I was also never really that self-conscious about my voice. I was *always* a talker, and even the thought of not being able to speak sent chills up my spine. So I just ended up going with the tracheal shave. It cost $4,000.

I scheduled the appointment. It turns out there was this huge party the night before. Paris Hilton was releasing her new single "Good Time." It was at this club called Create in Hollywood, and my friends were taking me. We were out really, really, really late. Everyone was doing drugs. It was just a regular night out in Los Angeles for me, but I was out until about six a.m.

I had to leave by seven a.m. to get to the appointment, and I was *definitely* still fucked up. My friend Arika drove me and I was still totally hammered. But we went to the doctor's office anyway and checked in to my surgery.

I don't advise doing this, by the way. It's just what happened.

The nurses at the doctor's office told me I was the first operation of the day. I went in. I didn't have to change my clothes. They washed my neck and pulled my shirt down, and I lay down on a table. It was so scary and so cold. The doctor turned all the lights on and I saw this operating bed and these huge, huge lights hanging above it. I remember them flickering and turning on really slowly. Then I looked around the room at the operating tools. It felt a little bit like I was in a horror movie, about to be brutally tortured.

I could barely see anything while looking up at the bright lights and lying down on the table. I felt like I was still in the club, drunk and overstimulated. The nurse was by my feet and started rubbing my leg. I guess she could sense I needed to be calmed down. The doctor cranked the headrest back more so that my head was lower than my body and my neck was fully exposed in the air. It kind of felt like I was choking, but there wasn't anything on my neck. Then he injected me with this huge needle. It was numbing. I felt a prick, but then I felt absolutely nothing.

I thought I was going to be put completely out under anesthesia. I was like, "Hey, you're going to knock me out, right?" They said I was just going to be numb, but they'd inject me with more numbing serum or syrup or medicine or whatever the hell you want to call it if I needed it. And I felt like I was tweaking. It was just insane. Eek-a-*fuckin'*-deek.

I really thought to myself, *Am I going to die? What am I doing? I wouldn't have done this if I would've known I would be awake! Why did I go out until freaking six a.m. last night?*

When they do the tracheal shave, they cauterize your neck to open up your throat. It helps for seamless healing. I didn't know this was going to happen. They Velcroed me in and I could smell my burning flesh. It was a true nightmare. It burned as they worked on it for a little bit. It was really uncomfortable. It felt like there was enormous pressure on my neck.

They burned it. They opened it. They sawed it, I guess. I didn't hear a *zzz* sound or anything crazy. It was just kind of silent, to be honest. The doctor stitched it up from the inside. I think the whole process took an hour.

In all truth, I think the operation would have been worse if I'd been sober. It was totally terrifying.

After it was over, I was a little bit out of it, to say the least. Arika had waited in the waiting room (God bless her), and I saw her the second I was done. I remember putting on my sunglasses. I remember there was medication. Painkillers. I had forgotten to pick those up before the surgery, so we went to the drugstore and got the pills. She dropped me off at a hotel, the Standard on Sunset Boulevard. I ordered mac and cheese, because I thought it was soft enough to swallow and not damage my new neck. I took a pain pill and fell asleep for the rest of the day.

I stayed there by myself for a couple days. I didn't tell anyone. To this day, it makes Tiffany sick that I went through that recovery alone. She was one of the only people (besides Arika) I told I was doing this. I didn't even tell my dad. I thought he would've been too worried, and I didn't want to stress him out. I also didn't want to put myself in a situation where I had to use my voice, because I definitely thought it needed rest after such an invasive procedure, and I knew people would want to call me.

That was the first time I had undergone a surgery to become Gigi. I look back and think it's so crazy that I had the balls to do that. It's one of the scarier things I've ever done to myself. When things calmed down and the doctor said I could take off the intense bandages, I had this clear little medical tape on my neck covering the incision. He told me I had to keep it on for two weeks. I finally felt good enough to go out of the house and see my friends. I went to Barneys and got a blue-and-red Alexander McQueen scarf. Come to think of it, I could

The McQueen scarf I used to cover my neck bandage.

have just leaned in to some turtleneck looks. But the scarf spoke to me.

I tied the scarf around my neck. It was my new must-have fashion statement—for two weeks, at least.

Now that I had the neck I wanted, I focused on my face again. The $4,000 that the tracheal shave cost actually kind of broke the bank, so in order to pay for the facial feminization surgery (FFS) I dreamed of, I had to actively save. It was very expensive. Forty-four thousand dollars. So my shopping addiction was on the back burner for now.

I had asked Betty where she had had her face done, and she told me she had it done in Boston. I looked into a few other doctors. A lot of them had operated on older trans people, or, at least, those were the photographs that I found on their websites. Maybe they just didn't have the permission of the younger people who got facial feminization surgery to post their photos. I know I wouldn't want my doctors sharing my before and afters with the world. Regardless, during my research, it was sort of off-putting that I didn't see any-body I liked. I didn't see anyone who made me want to work with them.

But in this case I trusted Betty. I saw the final product right there in front of me. She was stunning. And her work seemed so natural. But it was hard to get an appointment with her doctor, whose name is Dr. Spiegel. We were look-ing into it in October or November, and we eventually had a Skype interview. We talked, but I couldn't feel totally set on a plan without talking to him in per-son. I wanted to have the conversation up close and personal. My dad and I ended up flying there to do it.

At this point my dad knew a lot of my story. It was really hard talking to him about it, but I finally felt comfortable enough to tell him I was transgender. I had told him I had been on hormones for months. And I told him I'd booked the FFS surgery and there was nothing he could do about it. He thought the surgery was a terrible idea and, just like the therapist I went to for my permission slip for hormones, said that I was already so beautiful and didn't need any surgery on my face. That I was wasting my time and money to mutilate my face for no reason.

At the time I thought to myself, *How the hell does it make sense that you always saw me as a boy and now when I tell you I want to be a girl, you tell me I'm already beautiful and don't need anything changed to look like one?* I couldn't wrap my head around it. I feel like parents just don't want to see their children change in *any* way for *any* reason, because, in their eyes, they're perfect. I get that. But he also knew I was going to do what I wanted to do, that I was going to do it with or without him. It had already been paid for. I had wire-transferred the money. I had my appointment date.

I told him, "Dad, this is what I'm doing."

"Gigi, I'm coming," he insisted.

He told me that he would come to Boston regardless of whether he agreed with the surgery or not. I wasn't totally aware at the time of what he was doing, the commitment he was making, what his actions were saying. I didn't realize the importance of it. I didn't realize how lucky I was to have my father there by my side. I look back and see a little brat. A determined and relentless brat, at that.

I FEEL LIKE PARENTS JUST DON'T WANT TO SEE THEIR CHILDREN CHANGE IN *ANY* WAY FOR *ANY* REASON, BECAUSE, IN THEIR EYES, THEY'RE PERFECT.

He has always been there for me: with the boobs, with the face, with the name change. And it's simply because he loves me. At the time I took it for granted. A lot of trans kids don't have anything close to that. God truly did bless me with the life I was given.

Actually, a lot of people in general don't have anything close to what I had growing up.

FFS was something I wanted. I really loved Dr. Spiegel's work, and that gave me confidence. And so did the fact that Tiffany and my dad came to Boston and were there to support me. After getting the hormones, the lip injections, and the tracheal shave all by myself, I finally didn't have to do this alone.

Dr. Spiegel showed me on Photoshop what I'd look like after the surgery. We decided that he'd do my forehead, lower my hairline, flatten my caveman brow bone, swoop in to make my nose flat, and then round off my chin. I was contemplating rounding my jaw off, too, but it would have been too much, I think. *That's* where I drew the line.

Rounding off my jaw was something I wanted to do because a lot of trans girls feel they have very harsh jaws. They want to get them softened to seem more feminine and less masculine. The last time I had been in New York I talked to Amanda Lepore about surgery, and I asked her if I should do it. She said not to, that I have a beautiful jaw. I was scared of looking completely different, too. She also told me that when I get older, my jaw would keep me looking young.

I'm glad I didn't do the jaw shave. I love my jaw.

Because old ladies have no definition and their jaws flow into their necks like a seagull or something. That kind of changed my perception a little.

I'm glad I didn't do the jaw shave. I love my jaw. Also, I have big ears. And my ears would've looked even larger if I'd had my jaw rounded. Not cute. Would've had to change my name to Dumbo Gorgeous.

Anyway, without changing the jaw, Dr. Spiegel's operation could happen all at once. He told me it would take seven hours. That's a long time; I sleep longer than seven hours a night. Think about it. You could watch a lot of *Keeping Up with the Kardashians* in seven hours. You could watch like four movies. You could go from L.A. to NYC and almost back again. *Phew,* I'm tired just thinking about it.

I wasn't scared in the weeks leading up to the FFS, but the fear found me the night before and the morning of. I remember Tiffany and I ordered room service that night. It was so surreal. It was like *Holy shit, this is happening, this is fucking crazy.* This was the last supper (because you're not supposed to eat or drink after midnight the night before your surgery). It also turned out to be the one-year anniversary of my mom's death the next day. I hadn't planned that at all, but I knew that she was up there watching over me.

At the time, I was filming myself for what I eventually knew would become a documentary, but I didn't really want to talk. I wasn't in the mood. All I could think was: *I'm not going to look the same after today.* We took a picture and knew it was all going to be changed after, that I would look very different. Tiffany later told me she was really scared for me, that she didn't know what to expect.

I told them when I woke up to "film everything." I just knew this was footage I'd want to have in the future, whether I posted it or not. That it was pure gold. And how often do you get moments like this in your life?

We had to wait a long time before the surgery. I remember we watched *Seinfeld* in the waiting room. I remember being injected in my vein with the anesthesia and just sitting there naked, except for my hospital gown and hairnet.

It finally was time, and the nurse came to grab me and wheeled me out of the room. I said, "I love you, Dad. I love you, Tiff!" And I could see my dad starting to cry as I was being taken away. I looked at my feet.

"Guys, I'm drunk," I told them. I saw lights everywhere.

"No, you're not," they replied. "You're fine. The medicine is just kicking in."

The last thing I remember was looking up at those oh-so-familiar lights on the ceiling while I was lying on my back. About to be cut open and mutilated.

Seven hours later, I woke up in so much pain. It was the worst headache of my life. My face felt like a balloon. I could barely see anything. I noticed the video camera in front of my face. If it was on, the red light would've been blinking. The red light wasn't on. I saw it wasn't recording and mumbled, "Tiffany, it's not recording," through my bandages.

That's the first goddamn thing I said after I got out of my seven hours of surgery.

"It's not recording."

I was really unnecessarily rude to the nurse, too. Poor woman. "Give me a fucking painkiller," I told her. I remember a doctor who was kind of obnoxious when talking about the after-care process. He was really loud. I told him to "shut the fuck up." I kept saying "Shut the fuck up" over and over. And the nurse started laughing. I guess this reaction was normal for her to see postsurgery.

I had to stay overnight. I got placed in an ambulance and driven over to another building. I honestly don't remember anything from the aftercare, just that I had pudding to eat and I went to bed and slept a lot.

I woke up and I had bandages all over my face and head. My eyes were black and blue. My nose was in a cast. The blood had fallen from my forehead into my eye sockets. I looked crazy. I was sad. I thought I'd really messed up my face. It took a month and a half for it to fully heal.

I didn't really do much during that period. I was depressed. Actually, I wasn't just depressed, I was *very* depressed. When I met Betty, she'd just recently had surgery done on her face, so I assumed it would be a pretty fast turnaround. It was even more discouraging when I'd healed enough that most of my face was at least presentable, but there was still so much blood in my eyes from the forehead surgery that I couldn't go out in public. And it was hard to see sometimes. I remember one time I was at the store picking up a few things (and this was one of the first times I had gone out of my house) and a kid walked by me and screamed because he saw I had completely red eyes. It was so embarrassing and scarred me from leaving the house again.

Initially, I allotted myself two weeks in Boston to recover. Tiffany had to leave early because she was in school, and my dad left, too. So I was alone for a little while. Honestly, I just walked around in a pretty low-key way. Worried that I was going to get recognized from my YouTube videos or randomly (just my luck) see someone I knew. I was texting guys a lot on Tinder out of boredom, sending them photos of me from when I wasn't all surged out and looking like a character out of *The Walking Dead*. That, and room service three times a day. So boring.

By the time I finally got home to Toronto, I was really down in the dumps. I was still lying low because of my eye situation. I couldn't look anyone in the eyes. On the trip home from Boston, I got a *lot* of stares. I knew that I looked very scary, and I had never wanted to transport myself from one city to another so bad. All I wanted was my bed at home. My safe zone. Even though it had been two weeks, I looked like I had *just* had surgery. My face was really puffy, and I had trouble talking because of the stitches in my mouth.

Before the operation, I had made such a big deal about the surgery. I told everyone. The people I'd told were all so excited to see me and hear how it went. But when I finally got back to Toronto, I wasn't ready to see them. I still had to hide. I saw a couple of my friends, but I didn't tell a lot of people that I was back. It wasn't like, "Gigi's home, let's have a party."

I didn't make videos at the time for my YouTube channel, either. Before the surgery, I had basically stocked up on videos because I knew I was going to be out of commission, but I still wanted to engage with my subscribers. I made like five or six of them, but when those ran out, I thought I was really in trouble. I wasn't a vegetable, but I wasn't presentable. I didn't look normal.

And all I could ask my family was "When am I going to be happy with what I just did? When will this blood just go AWAY?"

Tiffany, my brothers, and Dad didn't really try to get me out of the house. They were well aware that my face was messed up in a bad way. But a new Toronto aquarium had opened up and my brothers really wanted to go. I don't know why, but I finally felt up to it. I still had to cover my forehead scar with a large bandage in the cold Toronto weather, so I made everyone wear these Brian Lichtenberg hats that said "Homies" on them. Except I wore one that said "Cunt." Everyone wore their hats out of solidarity. It was my first big outing.

Before any of my surgeries, when I started transitioning, I would call everything "she." And on this trip to the aquarium, I had everyone doing it. Everything was feminine. "Did you get your drink? Where is she?" Or "She is so cute," about an article of clothing. I'd be talking about a coat, or an octopus, or even a boy. They were all "she." It sounds like such a small thing, and maybe even a dumb game, but it helped me.

My chin was still really swollen, and I didn't look like myself. Looking back at photos, it wasn't as bad as I thought. And it felt especially good that no one was making a big deal out of it. My family made it feel so much better.

The blood in my eyes started gradually fading. At that point I was really, really into capturing footage for my future documentary. One day, I was watching footage back and noticed, "Oh my God, there's barely any blood left in my eyes!" From there, things got better and easier for me.

I've never regretted actually having the surgery. I will say, however, that I'm such an impatient person that I wasn't realistic about the timing. It's something I still struggle with. I bit off more than I could chew when it came to the procedure. Three huge surgeries are a lot for one anesthesia moment.

The doctor never said, "Don't do all three," but given my lifestyle, it wasn't the best idea. It was a lot to take on. I am so glad it's over.

I GOT MYSELF MY FIRST PAIR OF BOOBS FOR MY TWENTY-FIRST BIRTHDAY.

I lived life on the Internet. Because of my job, I was always social and always posting pictures for my friends and my subscribers. I would post on Instagram to show my followers I was still alive, to make the best of the situation. I'll say it again: The biggest problem was that the blood-in-the-eyes thing was not cute. Sunglasses were my only option.

But do you know what was cute? The boobs, which came very soon after.

I got myself my first pair of boobs for my twenty-first birthday. It was the best birthday present I could've given myself. I could have waited, but I wanted to be extra about it. I knew that it was ridiculous, but it was my next step. It's funny to get your boobs done for your twenty-first birthday.

They were $10,000, a price that might seem high but is actually on the low end for Los Angeles plastic surgeons. I went to Dr. Linder in Beverly Hills.

Even after hormone therapy, I had always been flat. I'd always dressed up and not worried about boobs. I never stuffed my bra or was insecure about how small they were. I worked with what I had. I was obsessed with my butt instead.

Whenever I would dress up with my friends and we'd go out in Toronto, they'd say, "Oh my God, your butt is so big." I literally did nothing to make it big; it was just that way, maybe from diving all those years.

When I was thinking about transitioning, I realized that I loved the way boobs looked. I then became obsessed with them. They were so sexy. And I loved that guys love boobs. They get so much attention. They're part of a woman and, for me, they were part of becoming a woman.

Once I decided I was going to get boobs, I made my little brother, Cory, look at them online with me. First we Googled "breast surgeons" and "breast augmentations." And then we Googled "Beverly Hills" and "sizes" and "textures" and "saline" and "silicone" and "where to get the incisions."

Cory was made very uncomfortable by it. He even had a hard time looking at the screen. Why would I make him look at pictures of naked girls with me? Why would I make him picture *me* as one of those naked girls with fake boobs? But I thought it was hilarious. I also wanted a straight guy's perspective and a brotherly perspective at the same time. A perspective from someone I totes trusted. He also happened to be living at home, so we could do research together. It was fun. I got to push him. And he got to look at a ton of nice boobs. He acted like he was super-uncomfortable, but I knew that he loved it.

A naturally inquisitive person, he was particularly fascinated by the fact that a boob—a breast implant—could go in a male person's chest. We read all about the process and he got into thinking analytically about boob sizes. Every girl wants the biggest boobs they can go for. Or at least every girl like me. I was fixated on getting the biggest boob size ever. Cory thought I shouldn't go too big, because he thought it would make me look trashy. He was like, "Reel it back in, Gigi. Reeeel it back." He's very sensible and conservative. He didn't want me to look bad. He has that brotherly love for me, even though I'm definitely outrageous.

But I wanted them big. I thought the bigger they were, the womanlier I'd feel. I think I just made up that word, by the way. *Womanlier.* Autocorrect thinks I mean *manlier*! Definitely not, computer, get it together. But I had the money, so I just thought, *Let me do it the way* I *want.* I totes ignored Cory. I probably wanted something like 700cc, which is about a D or bigger.

But that wasn't possible. The doctor told me my chest could take only so much. We ended up with a perfect 425cc. That's definitely not pornstar-gross huge boobs. It's kind of in the middle of implant sizes. Since I had little to no breast tissue, mostly puffiness, I had to choose a size that would fit just right. I was bummed, but I think Cory breathed a sigh of relief.

Getting boobs was extremely painful. It was the most painful thing that I have ever done. And remember, I have a high tolerance for pain, *and* I've had a lot of work done. Break a nail or stub a toe, I'm really dramatic, but every cosmetic procedure I've ever had I've been able to deal with pretty fast pain-wise (it was the emotions getting me down after my FFS). Also, the painkillers help. Getting boobs, though, was excruciating for three or four entire days.

That's because I got them under my muscle, and the muscle had to stretch out. Because I was so athletic, my chest muscles were really, really strong and tight. People describe breast augmentation as having an elephant sit on your chest. It feels like that, and also as if a car ran over your chest, too. I was in so much pain and so sore, I couldn't even leave my elbows by my sides. All I could do was cry and whine to my dad.

But it was totally worth the pain. After a week I was definitely good to go, while still being somewhat cautious. And I was definitely excited to be going out with boobs. The first place I went was Bootsy Bellows, a nightclub in Los Angeles. That was my spot. I went there every single day for two years. It wasn't just a coming-out party for my boobs, it was also my birthday party. My outfit was so turnt: a BCBG sheer baby-pink bodysuit with a peplum leopard pink Marciano by Guess skirt.

In the beginning my boobs were a new shiny part of my body. Like an accessory. For sure, I used to flaunt my boobs all the time. I would be out at the club, and if someone asked to see my boobs, I would show them. I think they weren't "mine" for a while. They were like a toy for a solid year. I would whip them out and show them to anyone who wanted me to.

I remember driving home from Vegas one time with a friend and it was pitch black out. We were in the middle of the desert when a huge truck drove by. Two guys were driving it and we thought we'd mess with them. I turned on the light in her car and took my top off. They both couldn't stop staring and honking the horn. We literally almost made them crash. It was hilarious.

When I first got my boobs done, I'd also show them to my brothers all the time. I'd be hiding, waiting around the corner of their bedrooms to scare them without my top on. They would always scream and freak out and immediately look away. I thought it was the funniest thing. Maybe I jumped on them once.

"I don't want to see your fucking boobs," I remember Cory yelling at me, as I laughed maniacally. Obviously, I knew I was fully their sister and this was something they never wanted to see. Ever. I just thought it was funny.

My ex, who I'll talk about a little later in the book, never liked it when I was overly sexual and sexy. And eventually I got as uncomfortable with the idea of my brothers seeing my boobs as they always were. Today, I wouldn't show them, because it's just too weird. Now my boobs are private. They are finally *mine*.

Everyone's insecure, especially about their bodies.

I guess I could say I grew into my womanhood. I started to feel a little less insecure about myself. Even though it seems super-secure to whip out your tits, it's insecure to be so shameless. A cry for attention.

I loved bra shopping, too. It made me feel like a woman to have bras. I felt like I was sixteen again. It was really exciting at first. Even if my boobs never needed a bra because they don't really sag, I still loved having a huge collection of them. *Shopping addiction vibes.* Now I don't even typically wear a bra.

It's certainly been a process, but I've started to realize that what makes you a woman is just you. It's not about how you act or how you smell or how you look. That stuff is all a bonus. It's about the person you are inside.

Now my boobs are a part of me. They're just another part of my body. I look at them, sure. I'm amused by them. In fact, I recently had them augmented to 500c. Which is basically the same as I had before—just different placement and nipple size. Thank you, Dr. Garth Fisher!

GENDER CONFIRMING SURGERY

As you know by now, I'm a person who doesn't hold back with anything, and once I started hormones, I made a list for myself of surgeries and life goals. One of those goals was gender reassignment surgery. This used to be known as a sex change, but that phrase has fallen out of use and some see it as offensive. Whatever you call it, it's *major*, bitch.

Hormones put me on the path toward balancing out. I was more of a woman, more like myself, or more like I imagined "myself" to be. After that, it was all physical changes. I'd never been in a real relationship with someone. I'd never felt truly comfortable in my body. I knew that I had to change that to be happy. In the wise words of RuPaul, "If you can't love yourself, how in the hell are you gonna love somebody else? Can I get an amen up in here?" Love her.

I really want to emphasize the fact that every transition is different, looks different, feels different. No two people are the same. I didn't think I was going to be "happy" or "done" or "wanted by the opposite sex" or even "happy having sex" or all of those things until I had gotten rid of my penis and got a vagina. I looked at the girls I knew and thought, *Oh my God, they're so happy. They're so beautiful.* They were full cisgender women.

After getting the boobs, I planned to wait for the perfect time to finish up my surgeries. At the time, I was going out every single night, and I was having fun in my new body. I finally felt really comfortable and, girl, was I living.

My dad would call me from time to time and always seem to ask me, "Oh, well, when do you plan on getting the reassignment surgery? I obviously want to come to help you through that, too. Let me know the dates and location you're thinking of."

He kept asking. He was fixated on it. Every time we would catch up, he would say, "Any news on the gender reassignment surgery?" I felt like he thought this surgery would be similar to the others. I would go off in private, plan it all myself, and then, after it was done, give him the details. But even to my impatient, ADD brain, it felt more serious than that. Not something I was going to schedule in secret, on a whim.

I'd respond, "It's sweet that you keep asking, but I don't have any news on it yet."

I was living my life in L.A. I had fallen in love with this guy, and he didn't care that I didn't have a vagina. He actually loved my penis. I was having amazing sex with him, for the first time ever. It felt right. I didn't want to be on my back for another month or so recovering from *more* surgery.

But it was also really difficult to talk about this particular thing openly. Every time I would do an interview, people would ask if I'd had a sex change. I totally understand being curious about what's between a transgender person's legs, but I thought, *It's none of their business!* Especially when we're LIVE on the air in front of a studio audience! I mean, *gag!* It was just so awkward. I've always tried to duck the topic, to dodge the questions, to change the subject. My publicist has always said to avoid it because she knows it makes me uncomfortable, both the question and the surgery, and she helped me with ways to respond to these invasive questions.

"It's no one's business," she'll say. "It's also something people don't need to be worrying about. It's superficial and can make you look shallow, which you're not."

I used to be asked about the surgery a lot more than I am now, which I get, because sometimes my YouTube content would include references to the things I'd done to my body. I've been super-open about a lot of things that people don't usually talk about. You don't need to know if I pee standing up or sitting down, but I don't care. I'll tell you that I always pee sitting down; I was always a sitter. So I understand why it can seem like no topic is off-limits with me, but it's different when I'm deciding to share something personal versus someone asking me something personal. The most uncomfortable time someone asked about it was at an event I went to. I'd just posted a video about my boob job. This horrible reporter on the red carpet had a huge studio light shoved in my face and flat-out asked me, "So give us the exclusive! Do you have a penis or a vagina, Gigi?"

"I was actually *just* thinking of asking you the same thing, sir!" I quickly replied. "Actually, please don't answer that. That's really gross to think about. I don't want to think about what's under there." I gestured to his pants with a sour look but still managed to smirk and wink as I walked away.

I handled it well, but I was so humiliated I wanted to die. My publicist immediately asked the cameraman to cut out any reference to surgery before it was posted. But it made it really obvious that I didn't have the gender reassignment surgery, because if I had had it done, I would have been screaming it from the rooftops at that point. Just like I had for all my other surgeries.

The truth is: I'd never even had a consultation.

From what I knew, gender reassignment surgery is a full-on thing. It would cost about $50,000, depending on where I went. I knew someone who did it in Canada free of charge under the health care of the country, and another who had it done in Thailand.

It's not an easy thing to deal with physically. Your body sees your new vagina as an open wound and is constantly trying to close it and heal. It wants to close the vagina completely. You need to dilate or stretch out your vagina three times a day for twenty minutes with these large dildo-shaped rods put inside of you. It takes a lot of strength and discipline to follow through with this surgery, so I have a lot of respect for people who've done it. This may sound silly, but I couldn't see myself having the patience to do that, especially with how happy I was feeling at the time.

I think there's a stigma if you don't have the gender reassignment surgery. If you don't have the gender reassignment surgery from man to woman or woman to man, penis to vagina, vagina to penis, you can be seen as less than, especially among people who aren't transgender. But I've learned that that's the furthest thing from the truth.

Among people who identify as trans, the community is a little bit more understanding. A lot of people don't have the means to do all the things that I've had done, let alone go through with it. I know people who are dying to have a gender reassignment surgery, and they don't have enough money to pay for it.

Honestly, I've always felt insecure that I had a penis and not a vagina. Now I've been given a voice for the community and I still don't want to talk about it, but I'm going to, anyway. Because it makes people think you're less of a woman or less of a man, and that's unfair. And untrue. And super-frustrating.

Look, I have my days, for sure. A lot of them. Bad days. Depressing days. Days I don't want to get out of bed. Everyone's insecure, especially about their bodies. Sometimes I feel comfortable showering around my friends; sometimes I don't.

The only people I'm able to be completely naked around are Tiffany and my soon-to-be-wife, Nats. I learn to love my body a little more every day, but it took me all of the surgeries I've had to fully accept myself.

I'm in a relationship now. Sometimes, when I was single, I never really knew how to approach the issue of my body, or how it would affect my connection with someone. I thought people might be more judgmental, or completely write me off because of my penis. And I was definitely a lot more unsure of myself. It was a huge secret.

Sometimes, in front of friends or strangers, I would say that I'd had gender reassignment surgery. When I came back from getting my boobs done, to some people I'd just say, "I'm fully done." I felt good about lying. It made sense to people that I'd had the full surgery. Physically, of course, she has a vagina, they'd think. It gave me a feeling about having gender reassignment surgery without having to go through the surgery.

I also think people don't really have a sense of boundaries when it comes to asking about this sort of stuff, and I want to make something clear: You don't ask a girl if she has a dick, let alone if she has a UTI. But when you're openly trans, people think they have the right to know everything about your journey and your body. But some things are private, and you can decide what you do and don't want to talk about, and who you want to talk about these things with.

And another topic I'm sure you're wondering about: How do I feel about getting the surgery these days? I think it's hard to imagine having a vagina.

And I know now that it's such a personal decision. No surgery can change you. It's all about what's going on inside and what *I* want. If there ever comes a day when I want to get gender reassignment surgery, I will do it. I already have a few doctors in mind.

My dad is relieved for sure. It's another surgery he would have to go through, to be stressed about. Over the various wild things that I've done the last few years, he's continued to ask about it. And eventually I just said, "Dad, I'm going to do it when I want. Please stop asking me about it. I'll come to you when it's time."

I grew up so much after all the stuff I had been through. My dad now knows I'll talk to him about it if and when I'm ready. If I told him I never, ever wanted to get it done, he would be okay with that, too. He's pro–anything I want. I love him so much.

If I had to make a real proclamation about gender reassignment surgery at this exact juncture, I feel like I might be ready to get it in five to ten years. Part of me wonders if I'm holding on to my anatomy so that Nats and I can have children. Maybe I'll grow out of this, but at the moment, I don't want to adopt. I want my kids to have my DNA. It might sound shallow, especially since adoption is so beautiful, but I just think I will feel so connected to the baby who has traces of me, Nats, and my family members in his or her face and personality. It's definitely a part of why I haven't had the surgery. At least in that department, everything is working fine.

One other caveat: When you get gender reassignment surgery, you're taking a chance in relation to what you can really *feel* down there. With the current technology, I know girls who have a fully functioning vagina and can experience orgasms. But your body might not take to the recovery. There are a *lot* of cases where it doesn't work and it's just a new hole in your body. I personally know many girls who have had this happen, and it's a really scary thing. There's no feeling, there's no orgasm.

And I love sex way too much to screw with that right now.

HOOKING UP WITH GUYS

I didn't have a ton of experience "hooking up" in high school. I didn't really meet guys at school because there were only a couple other gay guys. It was Catholic school, after all. We would all walk around in our hunter-green uniforms like robots. There was Hank who I've already told you about. I didn't feel any pressure with him. I felt comfortable and so did he, which made it really easy.

I would meet guys around my hometown, but none of them really impressed me. Either hooking up was always awkward or I was just flat out not into it. I wouldn't really start dating until I started traveling for my job. I actually had guys in a lot of different cities. I'd always joke that I had "hoes in different area codes." Wherever I was traveling, I'd have a rolodex of people who lived there that I'd hit up. We'd go out to clubs, and I'd meet people, and we'd have more of a friends-with-benefits situation.

You might think I'd be confused about my sexuality, but really, growing up, I had a lot of confidence for the most part. I got a lot of courage from having such a public life online. I would get all these compliments from my videos, some of which involved me giving out advice. Just as I was making other people strong, they were making me strong at the same time. I look back on that time and wonder: How the hell did I do all the stuff that I did? I was so confident, it's crazy.

I honestly never had a serious relationship as a gay boy. I'd fool around and be promiscuous and slutty. I'd experiment. I'd hook up with "straight guys" all the time. Or straight-acting guys. Or maybe just straight-questioning guys. Whatever I did, it used to make me feel really feminine and they loved me.

I was always into "turning" guys. That means having gay experiences with guys who label themselves straight. I loved a good turn, bitch. Going to a gay club wasn't so fun for me. Even though I was a boy, even though I didn't know I was transgender then, it made me feel like less of a woman. My goal was to be more feminine. I knew I was special, I just didn't know exactly how yet. I guess being with a straight guy made me feel more feminine. If I went to a gay club, then I'd be like every other gay guy there. I felt I was something different from that.

When I started going out to clubs, I started getting really promiscuous. I started dabbling in makeup. It would give me a persona in bed. I would always be the submissive feminine one. I knew my role. It made me feel important to have guys treat me like that. I got so much attention.

The time I had my most crazy sexual experiences was definitely when I was going to college in Toronto. Like I told you, I never went to school. I would wake up and go to lunch with my friends, or go shopping, or film the reality show I was doing at the time, or just do nothing. My schedule basically revolved around my next date and lying to my parents.

"School's great," I'd tell my mom and dad.

"Come over to my apartment," I'd tell some random guy I'd met at a bar or a restaurant or just walking down the street. I was living really recklessly.

One thing I *would* always try to do before ever being alone with guys I had just met was let them know the truth about my situation downstairs. Most of the time guys would hit on me and think I was a girl. If I was interested, that's when I would make the decision to have "the talk" with them and tell them I have a penis. I never wanted to put myself in a situation where I was in bed with someone and they were shocked by what they saw. I know a few girls who live like that and I could never. Other times guys would come up to me and know that I was an androgynous boy wearing makeup. Those times I had nothing to explain. And that's when shit got the most freaky.

When the guy would come over, I would always pretend I was a girl. I don't know if I used a name like "Gigi" at the time. I don't remember if I ever even told them a name at all. I just remember telling these guys, these one-night or one-day stands, "Don't call me by my real name because it will ruin the moment." I wanted to live in a fantasy.

It shocks me to think it, but I never got into any *real* trouble with guys being as promiscuous as I was. I was never abused, never hit, never felt like I was in a potentially dangerous situation. Nobody ever hurt me. I'm smart, but I'm also lucky. The reality is, anything could've happened—at any given time. Looking back at younger me, I feel almost maternal and want to tell myself to be more careful. But I think it helped that I was up front about who I was and what I wanted and listened to my instincts about the people I met.

10

---◆---

THE HILLS ARE ALIVE

---◆---

reality check

Gigi wears a Paloma robe, Bobbi Brown Primer Plus Mattifier,
Make Up For Ever HD Foundation Stick, Make Up For Ever Full
Cover Concealer, MAC Studio Fix Powder, Anastasia Beverly
Hills Brow Pencil, Benefit Hoola Bronzer, Lilly Lashes Sydney,
Milk Kush Mascara, Givenchy Rouge Stiletto Lipstick

First trip to L.A., at the Best Western on Sunset Boulevard.

But on that first trip to L.A., I decided that I wanted to be famous. That was when my fascination really started, with the actual city and not the television version. There's a long drive from the airport to West Hollywood, and it was my first time in a big city seeing billboards that size up close. I was used to seeing them on skyscrapers in New York City. The people's faces on the billboards were so prominent. There were humongous billboards everywhere, and they kept going all the way up La Cienega Boulevard, all the way to the top of the hill. They hung so low to the street, you could see every detail. I fantasized about seeing my face up there. And what people would think when they drove by it.

I never thought it would actually happen.

(Spoiler alert: It did. When *This Is Everything* was released, it felt like I'd scammed the system. Suddenly there were posters of me that huge everywhere. I didn't feel like I deserved it. I didn't belong on a billboard! This was insane! But who cares? I got it.)

My parents were not the flashy types, so my mom and I stayed at the Best Western on Sunset Boulevard. I've passed by since and thought about going in. It's the one with the overgrown ivy across from the Andaz. At the time, I was so pissed about staying there. I wanted the five-star treatment. I wanted it all *Pretty Woman*–style.

When we were in L.A., my mom made me take the bus. I think she secretly liked seeing me pouting and uncomfortable. She got some weird satisfaction out of it and found it funny. That bus made me miserable. I wanted to ride around in a convertible with the top down and blast music, like in my dreams. If you ever live in L.A. you'll learn quick: Everyone drives everywhere.

I wasn't very prepared for my appearance at the Abbey that day. I hated my outfit. I wore these really ugly oversized gray shorts and these hot-pink shoes I had bought the day before. Yvonne took me to Santee Alley downtown, where everything was *so* cheap. I had to memorize ten beauty tips about how to stay gorgeous during the summer, demonstrate them, and do a speech in front of a big group.

But this was the Abbey, one of the most famous gay bars in the world, so there were a lot of sweaty gay boys around, and we had to walk through them to go to the event. I felt like I had entered an alternate ultra-gay-sex universe when I walked through the front gates. Once we got inside, it was a completely different crowd made up of a bunch of influencers, media outlets, and fans.

Despite one or two slip-ups during my speech, the appearance went well. Yvonne seemed happy, and I had a *blast* on my first ever real job out in L.A. I could tell that my mom was really proud of me, too. On the way out of the Abbey, there was a tall man and his daughter waiting for me. She was underage, and the bouncer wouldn't let her into the club. She was crying and so excited to meet me. Sure, there were a lot of people inside during my speech whom I had taken photos with, but there was something about this young girl in particular. She asked me for a photo, and I hugged her and her father. That made me realize maybe I could be famous in Los Angeles one day. Maybe I wasn't so far off from Lauren Conrad and Heidi after all.

The whole thing was so turnt. And I felt like I wanted to do more of it. I thought, *This is what celebrities do every single day.* They do appearances, and it's so fun. I believed in the product I was promoting at the time, too. I really did use Lashem every day, and loved the results! The cherry on top was that I got to meet up with followers I would've never met if it weren't for Yvonne's invite to California. I saw that I had followers outside of Toronto. It was such a moment. The Internet had more reach than just to my school and to my neighbors. It reached across the country, maybe even the world. It was crazy.

When we left, I thought to myself, *This is where I want to live, and I wanna be really, really successful.*

At Beautycon 2013, one of my favorite events to go to!

I came back the next year for another event, at the Make Up For Ever store on Robertson. I was still Gregory Gorgeous, but this event was bigger. I traveled with a mini-entourage this time: my manager, Scott, and a videographer named Stefan. We'd all worked together on this Toronto reality show called *The Avenue*. I had to make my favorite picks of makeup at the Make Up For Ever counter. There's a video of this, too, so you can be sure it happened. Back when I was into the short blond bob vibes.

The day of the event, there was a huge poster of me and a line out the store. I signed autographs and took pictures. I remember going to Kinkos to print flyers of myself, and we stayed at a hotel in the Valley. Like, girl . . .

It was a trashy hotel and I didn't even know what the Valley was at the time. Everyone always talked badly about it. Like all, "Ew, the Valley" or "She sounds like a Valley Girl." I just knew that we were far away from the action, and we had to take the highway anywhere we wanted to go. We shared a room, too.

I really didn't care, though; at least we were all in L.A. together, doing what we love and having a blast. But I knew in my heart of hearts that this was temporary and it would eventually change.

The next time I came out to L.A. I was with my manager Scott, and we stayed at the Andaz Hotel in West Hollywood. That's when I started going out to the club and meeting the friends I have now. The stuff that I was doing started to feel, well, glamorous. I was making YouTube videos all the time. But,

BUT WHEN I LANDED IN L.A., I WAS GIGI. NO QUESTIONS ASKED. NEVER A PRONOUN MIX-UP. NOTHING.

behind the scenes, I learned that it's not all glamour. For instance, whenever I was on set, I usually had to wait in a dirty room in the back for an hour before I got to be a part of the action. And the final product would look so glamorous on-screen, but while shooting, it seemed a little whack. People are late and you have to do your own face makeup and your own hair. Meaning, the glam doesn't come the second you get off the plane in L.A. You have to earn it.

Still, I knew that I didn't want to live in Toronto anymore. I was over it. I had spent my entire life there, and sucked the city dry of everything it had to offer me. I felt it was holding me back. When I decided to become Gigi, I was also really trying to get away from my old name and my old life, which didn't fit me anymore. I would still keep in touch with my old friends, like Sierra, Marc, and Victoria. I didn't cut them off, but I knew that I needed a fresh start.

When I started coming out to L.A. more frequently, I was in a feud with my dad. He saw me as having two identities: Gigi and Greg. He struggled with seeing me as all Gigi. My friends were hundo P on board with the change and my dad wasn't. But when I landed in L.A., I was Gigi. No questions asked. Never a pronoun mix-up. Nothing. No one had met me as Greg. People might have known about my past, and of course they knew that I had one, but they didn't see it up close and personal. I was just Gigi to them.

It was so freeing knowing that a mere five-hour plane ride from Toronto to Los Angeles could bring me happiness and let me be the gender I wanted to be.

My dad had other reasons for not wanting me to move. He was scared about the long distance. He'd heard so much about the bad parts of L.A.: the drugs, the overpartying, the rehab. He was nervous about me crashing and burning and wearing myself thin. He always wants the best for me. But I did it.

And by the time I moved, I was pretty comfortable with L.A. and vaguely knew my way around. Right off the bat, I noticed there were definitely more gay people there. I had amazing friends in high school, but in L.A., the first people

I met were gay. It felt like people there were more accepting, more open. There was also a lot of sexual fluidity, something I didn't expect. Male models would hook up with each other, and girls would be with a guy one night and a girl another. All in the club. It was shocking, but I loved how free it felt.

As weird as this sounds, I also always felt more like an L.A. person because I was blond. One of my goals in life has been to be blond and tan forever. That's the L.A. look. When I met Amanda Lepore for the first time, she told me, "You're so L.A." I didn't know why she said that or what she meant exactly, because she was blond, too, and she lives in New York. But she was right, as usual.

L.A. felt like my fresh start. No one looked at my past. I mean, I'd put everything online for the world to see, but people in L.A. aren't known for doing "research." I was only Gigi to them. More and more, it was home. My real home. It was so refreshing to not have anxiety about being called the wrong name. For once people were calling me by my *right* name. The name I chose.

And besides, it was fun. Like, super-fun. More fun than I could have ever imagined. In L.A., there's a party every day. I loved how fun that was. I loved the attention that I got when I dressed up. I loved how accepting everyone was. I loved partying and looking cute. You'd go out every night and meet someone different. I loved meeting celebrities. I loved partying with celebrities. My teenage self would die inside *every freaking night* if I told her the things I'd be doing when I grew up.

I guess I should talk about my partying ways. I'm not trying to be a role model here. After my mom died, I turned my dad's house in Toronto into party central. I would always have people over. Drinking and partying. Loud music and smoking cigarettes. I would always entertain. But at a certain point in the evening, I would get very forceful and say, "Where are we going out?"

I love going out. Even in Toronto, I had a fascination with doing my makeup the craziest way possible and putting on the highest heels. Toronto wasn't so much my scene. But when I lived there, we'd go to this all-nighter club called Guvernment a lot.

Los Angeles can be kind of isolating, and maybe that's one of the reasons it's really a going-out town. When I moved there for reals, I kind of got into a cycle of going out only at night. I would always have plans. And if you go out all night, you end up sleeping all day. I would film, stay home in my cave, and edit. Then I'd get ready and go out and party crazy all over again, and then edit the next day.

A lot of friends I made in L.A. were "nightlife friends." We would get a group of ten people together, at about ten p.m. We would *always* do a dinner, but it would be a dinner where no one would eat. It was basically a waste of a dinner reservation because we would all have only a couple cocktails. The poor chefs in L.A. Never getting to actually *make* the decadent food on their menus.

It won't be shocking to hear, but in L.A. people care about the way you look and your body. Everyone was ultraskinny and ultrapretty. I once heard that Los Angeles is a place where all the best-looking people from each small hometown across the country live. This is a true statement.

I never really had "body issues" in the way that people talk about body issues. I never had to worry about my weight. The only thing I wanted to change was to make my body more feminine. But L.A. set up a whole new level of beauty. It can be intimidating. I was influenced a little bit by it, but I always had a sense of independence, and I knew I looked different and my body was just fine.

It won't be shocking to hear, but in LA. people care about the way you look and your body.

Anyway, at these dinners we'd get drinks and eat a little bit (sometimes), and someone would end up getting the bill. I'd get it on occasion, but I'd always feel more feminine if someone else paid. In the club scene in L.A., it's important to show your worth, that you have money and that you are financially stable. We would go out for free every night. I never had to pay for a single drink anywhere. I never paid to get in to any club. From when I landed in California, I really was treated like a celebrity thanks to my amazingly gracious friend Markus Molinari, who owned a lot of the cool spots around town.

Of course, in L.A., there's a level of fakeness. A lot of the people I met were kind of plastic and superficial—physically and personality speaking, that is. Whenever there are celebrities, drugs, and free shit around, you would be surprised by the things I've seen. Someone would be talking shit about someone. Absolutely no loyalty whatsoever. That's why I started to group people in my mind as my "friends" and my "nightlife friends."

"Nightlife friends" were people I saw only at the club. People, for all I knew, who just talked behind people's backs and leeched drinks off of the latest club promoters. People I really knew nothing about, and really didn't care to know anything about. I didn't care to ask where they grew up, who they were dating, what they did for a living, because I didn't trust them. I didn't want to share anything about myself, either. I stand by that saying—once someone shows you who they really are, believe them. (It's Maya Angelou.)

My manager and I would always talk about that. Remember, we're from Canada: land of the honest and overly nice humans. We had good heads on our shoulders.

In the beginning, going out is kind of what made me known. I love taking cute pictures of myself, and I'd always post them on my social media. But eventually, paparazzi started following me, too.

There was this YouTube channel called PopCandiesTv, and every night they would upload these paparazzi videos of me outside Bootsy Bellows on YouTube. Mine would get lots of attention. People thought I paid them to follow me. I swear on my life I didn't!

Because I'm a smart-ass businesswoman, I capitalized on that. Every day I would watch the video, download it, and re-cut it to music. I'd share it with my social media following. I'd promote the videos, and PopCandies would see I had pull on YouTube. My videos would have more likes than a red carpet video of Angelina Jolie at the Oscars. Then the PopCandies people would continue to follow me. So it was a self-fulfilling prophecy that in turn made me look more successful.

This would happen every single night of the week. Or at least five out of seven.

I think before I moved to L.A. for real and didn't have my own apartment, the town seemed like a playground. Balancing work and play wasn't a problem. But living in the city, this was actually my life. And suddenly every day was a vacation.

I was drinking a lot. Yes. Endlessly. There were shots all the time. A lot of alcohol. And drugs. I was doing coke. There was always coke. Sometimes the hangover was really bad, and I would swear I was never drinking again. Until the sun set and I decided, "What's one more night of fun?"

I knew things were starting to get out of control. The month before I moved, I shot a campaign in Canada for Crest toothpaste. They told me it was going to be in every Shoppers Drug Mart in the country. It wasn't a game anymore. I knew I needed to reel myself in. I needed to protect myself and my future.

The pressure was on. I didn't want to fail and have to move home. I was good at balancing but, Was I good *enough*? In L.A., it's always play, play, play. And I knew I had to play less and work more if I wanted to see it through with becoming Gigi.

11

---◆---

RELATIONSHIPS ARE GREAT UNTIL THEY SUCK

---◆---

so over it

The first time I hooked up with a girl was in New York. I'd just started my transition. I hadn't had any surgery yet. Nothing like that. I was only on hormones, though I started to change my identity.

A group of beauty girls were flown by YouTube to New York to be on a fashion television show. I was one of them. The first night we checked into the hotel, there was a welcome dinner for us all to mix and mingle, since we were from all around the world. The girls were sweet and absolutely beautiful. We had a couple drinks out on the terrace. They all had their hair and makeup done impeccably. Everything was going fine until I decided to use the restroom and this cisgender girl followed me in.

She was super-drunk. But she was flirtatious. "Let's pee," she said in a whiny voice.

She pushed me into a stall with her. All I could think was, *What is going on?* She went to the bathroom in front of me. It was so awkward. I wasn't used to behavior like this from strangers, unless it was at a club at one in the morning. She stood up afterward, without her bottoms on. There was a red heart tattooed right above her waxed vagina.

"Oh my God," she said. "Let me see your boobs."

I had hormone boobs at the time. I was wearing a floral chiffon top, and without asking or waiting for a response, she pulled my loose top down and started licking them. Needless to say, it was all a little much, and I didn't feel turned on at all. My boobs were so sore to begin with, let alone with her licking them. I remember cringing and looking up at the ceiling and mouthing, *Oh my FUCKING God.*

"Why don't you give my heart a kiss?" she asked, looking up at me.

I don't know what on earth came over me, but I just thought, *Why not? Why not give her heart a kiss?* And I fully ate her out in a bathroom stall. She stood above me like my master and I sat there kneeling. I opened my eyes and just stared at her heart tattoo. I felt sorry for the girl, wondering if I was doing it right. My knees were so uncomfortable on the tile floor.

We went back to the table and acted like nothing happened. Well, I did. She was kind of all over me that night. Eventually, I went back to my room and slept alone.

Over the course of the next week, we never talked about it or hooked up again. It was a confusing experience. In the moment it was kind of exciting, but after the fact I felt a little traumatized. It's not that I didn't like eating her out, it's just the way she went about suggesting it. It was a *lot*. She bullied me into hooking up with her, if I'm totally honest. It was fucking weird, but at the same time—and I'm not at all advocating for anyone to bully anyone else into hooking up—it was also kinda fun. I know it sounds like I'm contradicting myself, but that's what I'm telling you, I had these two different reactions to it! I remember telling Marc about it and saying, "It sounds a lot crazier than it actually was." He was *gagged*.

The truth is maybe I felt conflicted about the heart-tattoo bathroom incident because hooking up with guys is what I thought I wanted. I had this prehistoric notion that a man was supposed to be with a woman. I knew that I wanted to be the feminine one in the relationship. I'd only had mediocre to semi-good experiences with guys, but being with guys always made me feel more feminine because they were, well, guys.

When I was in L.A., I thought about hooking up with guys a lot. I thought it was important, because everyone else thought it was. Being one of the only transgender people in my close group of friends, we didn't frequent a lot of gay clubs. We went to straight clubs that happened to attract a lot of gay people, too.

The girls we would go out with would get attention from guys. Because of that, I felt like I needed and wanted that, too. I felt competitive. I'm a perfectionist, after all. Most of the time, I would go home after a night out totally alone. I'd take everything off and get ready for bed. My apartment felt like my safe space. I didn't let a lot of my platonic friends see me during the day, without my full Gigi makeup on. L.A. felt like a playground to me, but it also felt like a stage, where I had to be "on" all the time.

Maybe even then I was two different people, going-out Gigi and at-home Gigi. I suppose that has been true throughout my life. I did it to protect myself. To keep myself safe. I didn't see my "going out" friends as real people all the time. There was the nightlife and then there was real life. And at a certain point, I started to feel unbalanced.

There were several nights I'd come home from doing drugs and I'd be alone with my thoughts. I'd wonder: *Does anyone really care about me here in Los Angeles? Am I ever going to be with somebody, or am I going to be alone and isolated all the time?* Drugs made me feel weird. I never liked the come-down from the coke. It alters the way I think. And, honestly, I often felt relief just being by myself. I was away from all the pressures of performing or acting. I thought it might let people down to get to know the real me. I'm not *really* as feminine as I portray myself to be all the time, or as graceful, or beautiful, or funny. I put on a mask I could use to turn into someone else. A shield from the real world. If you want to call Los Angeles the real world, that is.

But I'm also hard to please. I get bored very easily. Guys were boring, or not enough. I'd be interested for a week or a month and then I'd get over it. I think, ultimately, I didn't want to be vulnerable. I had no reservations about hooking up, but having someone sleep over? Having someone experience the *next day* with you? Having someone see you with no makeup on? That I couldn't do.

USUALLY, I WAS THE ONE BEING CHASED AFTER.

I really tried from the start to be smart about hooking up in Los Angeles. It's a big place, but it's also very small. Word travels fast. I'd always heard people talking shit about each other after hooking up with them. People talking about "sloppy seconds." It was like high school, but a heightened version of that. People would say, "Oh, be careful about so and so," and I was very wary of being someone's gossip item.

I did make a few mistakes, particularly when it came to one-night stands. I would go to clubs, then afterparties in the Hills, huge mansions on top of Mulholland Drive with intimidating shark tanks. I'd get home at five or six in the morning. Or seven or eight or nine. And I'd bring guys home with me.

Usually, I was the one being chased after. Mostly by straight guys, which I liked, because a straight guy being into me made me feel pretty and feminine. I kind of relied on that feeling. As you may remember, I've always been drawn to "turning" guys, but I also don't like that I did it. It's an ugly term for me, because it means you're being dishonest with yourself and with the person you're "turning." And in case you haven't figured it out already, I'm a very honest person. A lot of my transgender friends love turning people. They get a sense of power from it. I get it. That kind of attention made me happy because I hadn't had that for so many years of my life. It gave me a fix, like stealing or spending money did. But being dishonest didn't make me feel good. And one was always entangled with the other. They were always two sides of the same coin.

A lot of my trans friends would not say they were trans until they got into bed with someone. I couldn't do that, because it would make me feel unsafe. Yes, I'd found myself in uncomfortable situations where people reached down to my genitals and reacted with surprise based on what they found, like "Whoa." But I didn't like it to get that far *ever*. I always tried my hardest to be honest and open, while still being desirable.

I would always try to make it known early on that I was trans. I would always make a point before everything got to be too much, before we got too far. If someone was kissing me out at the club, that's one thing. I couldn't help that. But as soon as it got further along, I didn't get off on them not knowing I was trans. I got off on the attention that was radiating in my direction. If they were still into me after they knew the truth, great. If not, *goodbye.* I don't need you.

But guys in Los Angeles were so openminded. We talked about guys being "straight but down," meaning they were straight but "down" to be with whomever. Coming from Toronto, where I got rejected a lot, this was refreshing. In Toronto, people were a) insecure and didn't want to be seen with someone transgender or b) less interested in me than I was in them. And as you know, a) I can't and b) I won't. Like this guy Brad. I liked him for a really long time. He was straight and we ended up hooking up. He became absolutely obsessed with me and we had a thing going for a long time. I thought we would eventually date and that I was going to be able to sustain it, but it wasn't great for my self-esteem. He would hide me from his friends and brother, while I was more than willing to invite him over to meet my mom. I had to end it.

I LOVED GOING ON DINNER DATES AND BEING PAMPERED AND CHASED AFTER.

In L.A., I felt really hot. The guys I met were cool with me being me. They didn't seem embarrassed by a hookup. I had full-on sex with someone probably once a week, if not more. I loved going on dinner dates and being pampered and chased after. I was always submissive. While I didn't like being put in a box as a one-night stand, I also didn't quite want something serious, and most of these encounters turned out that way. I definitely had a type: a guy who was taller than me, muscular, and had dark features. These were guys who could make me feel like a girl. Who'd make me feel pretty or feel wanted or feel feminine.

I even went through a phase of having threesomes a lot with one of the friends I talk about in the Cast of Characters section of this book. I'll let you decide who you think it is.

But eventually all the fooling around got to be too much. It felt dirty. I realized I couldn't be partying and sleeping around all the time. It got to be wildly out of control. To the point where many times I would wake up and not know where I was or who was in the bed next to me. Awful. L.A. was too much of a playground. I needed to be in a relationship. I wanted a boyfriend.

My ex and me in Pennsylvania.

I met my ex-boyfriend Cory B. at my friend Nick's birthday. I was twenty-one, just a few months after I had gotten my boobs done. He was tall and muscular. A military type. We made out all night long in the dark back room of Bootsy Bellows. The lights came on at two a.m. and I turned my head and he was there. And suddenly he was like, "I need to take you on a date." The fact that I was trans was definitely on my mind. Did he know I was trans? Was this a fetish of his? I thought he was cool enough and that I should give him a chance. Only one way to find out what his deal was.

So we went on a date. To this place called the Church Key, on Sunset Boulevard, not far from the Best Western where I first stayed with my mother. We talked all night. It was super-fun. He made me laugh. We went for a walk outside, and he bought me a rose. We ended up at the Mondrian Hotel, where we lay on the terrace, making out. At the end of the night, he called an Uber and dropped me off at home. (He lived only five minutes from me.) He said he really wanted to come up and hang out more. He was begging me. I told him he had to wait, and I'd see him later.

He ended up totally sweeping me off my feet. He didn't identify as gay, which made me feel good, and he was completely open about my identity and wanted to make me his girlfriend. It was a few weeks before we became fully intimate. I waited until I didn't think I would get hurt, when he wasn't going to reject me for being me.

I was really focused on my work at the time. I knew that if I was going to let anyone in, it needed to be for the right reasons. I really wanted a boyfriend, yes, but I also thought I had to make him work for it. I don't know how it all happened; it just happened. It was definitely meant to be during that time period. I'd heard that he'd had some experience with guys, but he said he didn't. I chose to believe him. We hooked up, and he didn't seem to care. I'm not really sure how he identifies now.

We dated for a year. A solid year. It was unlike anything I'd had in my life before. He ended up moving in with me. I was living in a one-bedroom at the time. He was working as a valet driver, totally content with that. Admittedly, I was a little embarrassed by that. I felt like I should be with someone with bigger goals. Still, I stood up for him because I loved him. At first I wasn't bothered that I was cover-

ing the rent, that I was paying for our lives, that he liked to party a lot. I just liked the idea that this cute guy I was having a blast with wanted to be with me.

It turned out I actually loved being in a relationship. I was so excited to have him come home for my dad's wedding. (My dad remarried the summer we were dating.) I couldn't wait to introduce everyone to my new boyfriend. But it was an awful experience. We landed in Toronto and Cory B. just ended up drinking a lot and slept in for the whole day of rehearsals. My dad was like, "What's going on with him, Gigi?" He had no respect for my family, and it showed. He didn't care. I was a bridesmaid, which was a huge moment for me, and Cory really put a damper on that day for me. But it was very easy to turn a blind eye to stuff like that. Just being with him made me feel protected. Which is ironic, because I'm sure being with me made *him* feel protected in many ways.

Cory's younger brother is a drag queen named Alaska Thunderfuck. Alaska had won season two of *RuPaul's Drag Race: All Stars.* And I think Cory was excited by his brother's "fame." I saw how it made Cory's eyes light up, and he reacted in that good, pure way to my successes, too. But all Cory wanted to do was party. We started partying a lot together. I would want to stay home, to do something normal like edit a YouTube video or put together furniture or do something domestic. Or maybe I was just tired.

Whatever it was, he'd figure out a way to change my relaxed and easy homebody plans. And we'd have the exact same kind of night in that we would have had out. It didn't feel right to me. I wasn't sure I could keep up that kind of lifestyle.

Cory was sometimes abusive emotionally, too. We were at a Wendy's drive-thru one night, toward the end of our relationship. We were in a fight at the time. Probably about partying too much or money or going out or my work. It was always one of those things.

I don't know what made him say this, like I'm not sure what we were really arguing about, but he said, "I'm giving up a lot by being with you." I wasn't sure what he meant at first. But he told me I needed to respect him.

"I'm with a trans girl," he added. "You know, a lot of people wouldn't say that out loud."

I knew that he was showing his true colors. It was the most abusive point of view he could have, one of the most insensitive things he could say to me. He was saying that being with me was somehow a negative for him. It made me feel as if I was less than a person.

Of course the signs were there all along. I just didn't really want to see them.

He would rage at me. He would ask if I was fucking someone else. He would play the victim and act as if I needed attention. He would suggest that I deserved the way he was treating me. He basically took over my life. My friends were bad for me, he said. He made me stop talking to certain people. He'd call some of my girlfriends "whores." He'd say they were lying to me.

Everyone else recognized his negative behavior before I did. Nick would say, "Cory is not a good person. We're just around him because you like him." I didn't notice it at all.

My friends would try to take me out and get me out of this thing I was in, this trap. I had really supportive friends. But I rarely went out with them alone. They'd say, "Girl, you deserve so much better than him." But whatever insecurity was plaguing me really did a number. I didn't believe I deserved any better.

It took me at least six months of being with him before I started to get the hint.

I think he had fully brainwashed into me thinking I wasn't worthy of being with anyone else. That I was going to be alone for the rest of my life. That no one else would want to date me because I was trans.

That's something that I never felt before, though of course, like many people (not just trans people), being alone was a big fear of mine. And he reinstated it. He slowly but surely took away my confidence.

It was confusing. He was always really funny. He was extremely easy to get along with. He didn't take life too seriously. But then he would turn around and talk down to me. He would make me feel like shit about myself. I knew, in the deep recesses of my mind, that he was a lowlife. After he put me down, I totally could have said to him, "You're a valet driver." But I never did.

I wasn't faithful to him. I realize now that I was trying to sabotage the relationship. Here's how it happened.

Cory B. used to work late nights. On one particular night I knew he'd be working till at least ten p.m. I had gone to the salon to get my hair blown out. I stopped at the gas station afterward to fill up my rental car, which had a Nevada license plate.

I love a cold-turkey moment. When you just quit something and that's it.

This guy who was also pumping gas near me asked if I was from Vegas. And we sparked up a conversation. He asked me to dinner. I said no, but we exchanged numbers. We texted for a while and eventually he convinced me. We went for dinner in the Valley. We talked the whole time. We just flirted.

I figured I'd be home in time for Cory. So I left my phone in my purse. It was only after we finished dinner—about eleven-thirty—that I noticed that Cory had been texting and calling me off the hook.

On the way home, I changed the guy's number in my phone so it looked like it was my friend Remi's. When I finally got home, I told Cory that I'd been having a girls' night out with Remi. He was pissed. I brought my phone with me to the bathroom and texted the guy to make sure he'd stop texting me. In

At a Dodgers game. Hate sports but love the merch!

the process, I accidentally left my phone in the bathroom . . . and Cory found it when he went into the bathroom after I did.

I only realized it when I heard him screaming my name from the bathroom. He was seeing weird texts from "Remi" on my screen. And, of course, he didn't believe the texts were actually from Remi.

So, I was doing things that were destructive to the relationship behind Cory's back. But maybe it was also my way of trying to end things without having to actually confront him with the idea that I was finished with him.

I think I did things like that on purpose because I knew what we had wasn't right. I was literally lying to myself. We would get into more fights, but he would always let me get away with what I'd done. It was probably because I was keeping him afloat financially.

I would pay for a lot. His gas. Our dinners. The rent at the apartment. I'd get him gifts, designer shoes and clothes, even though he didn't really care about brands. In fact, he was always on me for spending too much money on designer handbags. My reaction to that would be, "Who are you to tell me what I can and can't spend?" It's one thing for him to be like that when he's actually pulling in the bucks, but how dare he do that when I'm the one paying for everything?

I think the undercurrent of all of it was that being with Cory made me feel normal. I had gotten so used to having him around that I was afraid of what it would feel like to not have that safety net. I was the girl and he was the guy. We'd go to things together as a couple. We'd have sex regularly. What if I was never able to find that again?

The sex was fine. He consumed a lot of protein powder, so sometimes it was like he was on steroids. He would have spells of being really horny. Really horny. And he'd want to fuck five times a day. And he used to make me feel guilty when I didn't want to have sex. I found the sex to be a little been there, done that. I was more excited about my relationship. About being with a guy openly, about being in a real partnership. I was definitely more in love with the way we looked than with the way we felt.

At that time I'd really hit a groove with my work, I was a career girl all the way, but he even made me feel bad about working. He'd call me vain because I was going to get my lips done again. "Oh, it's the Gigi show," he'd say. He was jealous a hundred percent of my success.

But even though this was fulfilling a "heterosexual fantasy" for me, I had to come to my senses to realize that this was not what I wanted at all. I wasn't sexually happy, but, more important, I wasn't fulfilled spiritually.

And it was a completely "normal" "hetero" relationship, until he reminded me it wasn't at that Wendy's drive-thru.

I love a cold-turkey moment. When you just quit something and that's it. And that's how I ended things with Cory. It was for the best. I don't know about willpower, but that's how I did it.

Of course, I didn't feel great afterward. It was terrible. I felt so little. So small. I felt like everything I had worked for was crashing down. I was really down in the dumps. I felt like shit about myself. It was the worst I've ever felt. I had to really rebuild my self-confidence. I had to ask myself, *Who is this person? Who is Cory?* He definitely isn't the ruler of me.

The whole breakup made me question what I wanted. It put me in such a toxic place. I spiraled out, wondering, *Maybe I'm not ready for a relationship.* I'd wanted so badly to be with a man that this made me feel like maybe relationships are not for me.

The truth is, I was completely ready. I just had to start looking with new eyes.

12

FINDING MY MISSING PIECE

Gorgeous Star

I wouldn't say that being with my ex shaped who I am. But I would say it produced a stronger, more confident me. I needed to have that first unsuccessful relationship in order to be in the place I am right now.

As painful as it was, as much as it hurt me, I wouldn't change one thing about what happened. It made me realize my worth. And I think I'm worth a lot. Even at the beginning of my transition I knew that. I'm a good person.

I look back at my time with Cory B. and I'm upset that I felt I needed the validation of some idiot guy! Oh my God, he was the worst. Thankfully, I'm a fast learner. It woke me up to the fact that I didn't have time to waste. It taught me a lot about what might make me happy in the long run. A huge takeaway was knowledge. About myself, about what I needed for me. And I realized that focusing on loving myself was the most important thing. I didn't need to depend on a man or a relationship with someone else to make me happy.

My dates with guys after Cory were pretty lackluster. I would be out to dinner with someone who was handsome but also a brick wall. I know that part of it might be related to living in Los Angeles, where people tend to be more superficial and are interested in using you for your fame. But I knew that after Cory, I wasn't ready to commit to someone who wasn't on the same level as I was.

Dating a woman was never really on my mind. At the same time, I rarely enjoyed the sex I had with guys over the years. I liked flirting with them, yes, but once it got physical, it was hard to get excited. I've never been a huge fan of anal sex. A lot of times, as soon as I'd get into it, I'd be begging for it to be over. And I can't think of an instance where I really felt *connected* to a man in bed. But I just didn't look at women as romantic options.

That's partly because I lived as a gay man for a long time. As Gregory, I always thought my big relationship would be with a man, and that became true also when I began living as Gigi. When I transitioned, I thought I needed to be the most feminine I could be. I had in my head that I needed to be the epitome of a woman in what I said, what I wore, and who I dated. So dating a man would *confirm* to me and everyone else that I was a woman.

Around this time, after my breakup with Cory, I became good friends with August Getty, who is an awesome designer. Neither of us remembers how we became friends. Suffice it to say that we got really, really close really, really quickly. Before long we were having "filler" parties where we all had Botox and Juvederm injections at home, or burping contests, which I always won. He also started inviting me on lots of fun fashion trips. So at some point, he went to Paris to show his collection for Fashion Week, and he let me tag along. It was going to be a ten-day trip. He also brought his sister, Nats, whom I'd met before socially.

I didn't even know she was coming on the trip. We wound up spending every day together. Not just every day, but really every moment. Which was a lot more time than we'd ever spent together before.

On this trip, she confided in me that she'd always had a crush on me. During this initial conversation, she was extremely forward, openly hitting on me, making it known. It felt weird at first. I was overanalyzing it. Again, it

Now here I was coming out to them for the third time. First, I'd come out to them as gay. Then I'd come out to them as trans. And now I was coming out to them as a possible lesbian. They thought I was joking.

hadn't occurred to me that I might ever date a woman. I'd had this very strong idea of gender roles for as long as I could remember.

So there we were in Paris, far away from our real lives, a whole fairy-tale vibe. I thought the fantasy would evaporate when we got back to Los Angeles. Instead, I spent several nights at her house. We weren't sleeping together (yet). Eventually, at a place called

Nats and I on our engagement night at the Vaux-Le-Vicomte in Paris.

Club Sandwich, she kissed me. Soon after, I had to go back to Canada to work on my documentary. With some time on my own, I realized that maybe I had feelings for Nats, too. I had to sit and think. *What is this that we're doing here? Is this the beginning of a full-on relationship?*

Of course, I couldn't keep it a secret. I told my friends. They'd known me for so long, and they'd known me in my boy-crazy days. Now here I was coming out to them for the third time. First, I'd come out to them as gay. Then I'd come out to them as trans. And now I was coming out to them as a possible lesbian.

They thought I was joking.

Having had that challenging experience with Cory and how he felt he deserved a medal for dating me, I was worried about how Nats really felt about me being trans. I know how to own it myself, but the person I'm in a relationship with has to own it, too. I couldn't get into another situation that wasn't totally and completely public.

When I got back to Los Angeles, I really needed to have a conversation with Nats. We were hanging out with a couple of her friends, and one of them came up to me and said, "Do you guys fuck or whatever, even when you guys aren't blackout drunk?" Since that was one of Nats's friends, I wasn't completely sure that her heart was in the right place. I asked Nats the hard-hitting questions:

1) "How do you feel about me being trans?"
2) "Does it make you uncomfortable?"
3) "Have people brought it up to you?"

Nats answered my questions like a fucking boss. She took it for what it was. She was super-mature about it, understanding and sweet. She took her place as a part of the community right next to me, whereas my ex-boyfriend made me feel like being part of the community made me less of a person.

Nats knows that being trans is just equal, that I deserve everything anyone else has. I think it comes from the adversity she's overcome from being gay herself. She's dated men and women, but I think she dated men kind of in the way I dated Magda way back in high school.

The experience with Nats thus far has been so much different and so much more fulfilling than dating a man. The sex is great. I connect with her. Every day I unlock more and more things we have in common. I feel like in our relationship, I'm more feminine and she's more masculine. I mean, I do wear all this makeup, and I'm obsessed with getting glam. That's pretty feminine, I guess. Of course, she has feminine attributes, if it's fair to call them that. She's emotional, she's sensitive, she cares what she looks like. But I have masculine attributes, too. I definitely feel like I'm controlling and territorial. Though I would argue that being jealous is fairly unisex. Maybe more of these traits are unisex than we realize.

Marriage is . . . the ultimate symbolic step in love.

And I don't even know if it's a gender thing. Honestly, I feel as if it's just meeting the right person. At the end of the day, it's all about the connection.

I may be only twenty-five, but I've lived a lot. I've lived as a man. I've lived as a woman. And I know what I want when it comes to what makes me happy.

I had a very traditional upbringing. Family has always been really important to me. Ever since I was really young, I'd always wanted a husband or a partner. Now I realize it's about having the right person as your partner instead of looking like the image of "husband and wife" I'd always had in my head. And I always wanted a family with kids. Marriage is absolutely something that's important to me. It's the ultimate symbolic step in love. I've always wanted to be married. It's very traditional and romantic. It shows passion, and it shows the world you want to be with this person forever. But it's not only for the world, it's for the two people to know for themselves also.

I'm a firm believer that Nats and I will have a big wedding. A ring is great, but the whole thing is going to be mind-blowing. The ceremony, the speeches, the cake, the outfits . . . and the most important part: having the right person to walk down the aisle with.

FAMILY TO ME IS SOMETHING YOU CAN RELY ON THAT NEVER *EVER* GOES AWAY.

And since our engagement was already pretty over-the-top (see page 213), it's definitely going to be expensive.

I think that my relationship with Nats is the real thing. I might want to have natural children with Nats. We'll see. We have to get married first. And I've given a lot of thought to a potential wedding.

I MEAN, I LOVE TRADITION AND SHIT.

MY STILL TO BE COMPLETED WED

- Definitely have a four-day wedding.

- Get a huge, gorgeous custom engagement ring.

- Have my entire family there, and have all my and Nats's friends flown out to wherever we decide to have it (a destination wedding is suggested).

- Tiffany will be my best woman, standing beside me, but of course she'll have already helped me plan the whole event.

- Be expecting, or at bare minimum, I want the promise of a baby or babies on the way in the very near future.

- Have two secret things matching on Nats and me to signify the years we've been together. Perhaps our mothers' clothing cut up and sewn into our outfits, or words sewn on the inside of both of our outfits.

- Choose an epic location, maybe like the Malibu Getty Villa, to tie the knot (but a destination wedding is still suggested).

- Have a couple performances by musical guests that we each pick.

- All of our pets will have a part in the ceremony (i.e., Mr. Cat can be the flower girl).

- Look and feel the most beautiful I have ever looked or felt in my entire life on that day.

- Have an empty seat in the front row for my mom so I can see her from the altar, and if she doesn't have another event to go to, maybe she will join.

DING WISH LIST

- Have a gaggle of photographers and videographers to capture the entire day for my YouTube channel.

- Do a weekend getaway moment and have brunch and a beach/pool day with everyone the next day, after we tie the knot. (Remember, four-day wedding. Also, a destination wedding is suggested.)

- Have a dance with Nats's mom, Ari, after we are married, to her favorite song.

- Get a custom August Getty Atelier dress for the ceremony, and also a custom party dress so that I can change

into it after, when I want to be more comfy and have fun.

- Make Nats cry when I say my vows.

- Whisper something dirty in her ear when we are saying our vows on stage in front of everyone and about to kiss and make her laugh and feel embarrassed.

- August will do a secret performance (he told me to write that).

- Drive away in a vintage car at the very end with beer cans that say "Just Married."

- To be continued . . . (A destination wedding is suggested.)

P.S. I wrote this list while I was watching a wedding movie on an airplane.

THIS BOOK

HAS A

FAIRY-TALE

ENDING

We watched a lot of Disney movies when I was growing up, and I learned a lot of lessons from watching those movies. *The Lion King* was the first one I saw, but as you know, I truly related to Ariel in *The Little Mermaid.* Like me, Ariel was obsessed with water, and she wanted to be part of a world she didn't know a lot about. She gave up a lot to change her life.

When I look at my life now, I see my struggle in Ariel's. She didn't feel as if she was born with the right anatomy. She took a major risk in order to live the life she thought she deserved. I think she taught me well.

I don't know if I was always this way, but today I am a super-hopeless romantic. And I like using Disney movies as my guide. I like to think that Moana, Ariel, Esmeralda, Elsa, and lots of other Disney heroines give zero fucks. They live dramatically and authentically. They realize there's no use in being subtle about the way they live. They just do it. They go for it.

They just do it.

Hour to hour, I know that I'm living a real person's life, with the frustrations, struggles, flat tires, and broken nails that all of us deal with on a daily basis. But on the whole, when I step back and look at the big picture, I feel like my life is an extravagant, fantastic fairy tale. I get to travel all over the world— okay, minus Dubai. I get to go to amazing events. I get to live my dream life.

Even Nats's proposal to me was like a fairy tale. She brought me and my friends to a castle in Paris, via helicopter, that was like something straight out of *Beauty and the Beast.* Listen to her voiceover in that amazing proposal video, it was as if I was Belle and she was the Beast transformed. And when we danced in the ballroom, I could just hear Mrs. Potts singing "Tale as old as time . . ."

But what's more important, and what I think every Disney heroine looks for, too, is that I've been able to find my tribe.

I've got my tribe back in Toronto, where I'm so grateful to have my real family. And I've created my new family in Los Angeles. Family to me is something you can rely on that never *ever* goes away. And I look at all of them in my life and I wonder: How did I get so lucky?

Until next time, everybody. Stay gorgeous. XOXO

Me at the Vaux-Le-Vicomte.

THE MOMENT I SAID YES!!!

Taking a tour of Paris to the destination where I'd get engaged. Had no idea what was happening! LOL.

CAST
of characters

I have a big family. I have my family back in Toronto, and then I have my family of friends here in Los Angeles that I chose. We're all our own unique "characters," and we literally travel in packs. I can't go to a nail appointment without having five of my crew in the waiting area. They appear and reappear, but the fact that they are in my life stays constant. This can get confusing, so I figured I'd lay it out nice and clear for you.

I want to list all the important people so when you're reading, you don't have to say, "I'm obsessed with reading this book, hundo P, but I can't figure out who in the hell Gigi is talking about here. Which Marc is she talking about? Who's Sierra? What? It's confusing." This way, you can turn back to these pages and reacquaint yourself. Also, I don't think you can know the real Gigi without getting to know the people who populate my life and made me who I am today.

MARC   Marc is my best friend from high school, which means we've been friends for a really long time. He's the oldest friend I have. He's smart, witty, outgoing, and hilarious. We met in the sixth grade. So obviously we were in the same elementary school. We didn't like each other at first. We were both "straight" back then. Yes, I was "straight" in sixth grade, okay? We ran in the same circle and kind of saw each other as threats, I guess. We were pretty insecure back then, before we came into who we are now.

He came out of the closet before I did. When Marc said it out loud, I knew I had to do it, too. Maybe it was a competition at the time, but I think we were rooting for each other more than anything.

Marc is extremely out there and flamboyant. When we were younger, we were both very girly. One Halloween, we dressed up as an angel and a devil. He got his first pair of heels before I did, which made me go and buy a pair for myself. I actually always thought we would become girls together. But when we went on our own paths, he became more masculine, and I went in the opposite direction.

When I found out what it meant to be transgender and I spoke to him about it, he said, "That isn't me. But if you want to do it for yourself, I'm so down to support you every step of the way. Let's kill it."

He's the reason why I have my career. He pushed me to do YouTube in high school. It was never about the money. It was always just something he thought would be really fun to do. And he was right. It helps that our humor is exactly the same.

He lives in Toronto now, where he's extremely into musical theater and works as a tennis coach. He loves tennis. Tennis is one of his passions. I'm horrible at tennis but love the outfits.

SIERRA She's my other best, lifelong friend from Toronto. We went to the same high school, too. I love Sierra because of her infectious sense of humor. She really helped open up my inner class clown. We were (and still are) partners in crime. We used to be so bad, especially in math class. Our poor math teacher. I remember he strictly told us absolutely no eating in class. We would take Jamaican beef patty wrappers from our cafeteria, and while he was writing a lesson on the board, crunch them so loud and say, "Mmm, that tastes so good, can I have a bite?"

Sierra was one of the first people I told that I was trans. We also have matching tattoos of keys. I got mine on my left rib. It was all about closing an old chapter and opening a new one. She still lives in Toronto and works as a veterinarian.

VICTORIA This girl was truly a blessing in my life. Right time, right place. Her open and understanding heart always encouraged me to be my most authentic self. She and Marc were the best tag team to get me inspired and stay passionate. I'll never ever, ever, forget the unconditional love Victoria showed me. She just accepted me for me. I hope everyone gets to experience a best friend like that. God truly blessed me, starting in middle school, with a friend like her.

HUXCH Huxch, aka Nick, is one of the first people I met in Los Angeles. I met him with my friend Chris Crocker. We all met out at this bar in West Hollywood called Trunks. I thought he was gorgeous. We instantly clicked and have been friends ever since. I don't know exactly when or how, but I kind of look at him like my older brother. He is super-smart and creative, shows me unconditional love, and *always* looks out for my best interest. He's been a huge part of my life ever since I moved to California. We've been through some really crazy stuff together over the years. Breakups, achievements, family drama, you name it. With all the fake people who live in L.A., I really don't know how I got so lucky to have met such a genuine and real person so early. God really does work in mysterious ways, but I'll take it.

SCOTT Scott Fisher is my friend of almost a decade, and my manager here in L.A. Even though I'm still super-young, like a hundred years ago, when we were both living in Toronto, Scott reached out to me to do a reality show he was developing. He was a college student working at Starbucks at the time. He described the reality show he wanted to put together as a Toronto version of *The Hills,* and because I always thought *The Hills* was the best show on television, I was instantly in.

At the time, Marc wasn't as instantly convinced as I was. He said, "Oh my God, we need to make this guy Scott think we're more professional than we are if you're going to be on his show." So I made Marc email Scott as my fake manager. He wrote up these fake emails that said, "She is kind of interested, but she would need to be paid."

Scott was in college at the time and held castings at his apartment with his roommate Jake, so Marc and I drove downtown to meet him. I would always drive us in my mom's Volvo XC90. When I got there, it definitely wasn't the professional, up-pity setting I was expecting. It was me and these four other girls in this small room. We were the only five he met with, and we were the only ones Scott cast. We went on to film the show called *The Avenue,* which we all look back and laugh at now.

I like that Scott is very business smart. He gets shit done. When I started spending time with him, I saw he was a creative person. We got along. He got my sense of humor, and he always encouraged me to be as extra as I wanted to be.

We used to party crazy, crazy. But he decided he needed to stop partying as much as he did and start focusing on growing the business. He doesn't go out as much as he used to, but we've still remained close friends and business partners.

ADAM WESCOTT Now Adam is Scott's business partner. But originally, he flew Scott and me out to Los Angeles from Canada for this show he was working on called *Beauty Vlogger Bootcamp* with these hugely important beauty bloggers. Meaning: He gave me one of my first real breaks out in sunny California, and me and Scott one of our first trips together. He was the right-hand man on the set, and he liked my vibe. He still loves me even when I'm being a bad girl. If we get in a tiff over something—for instance, he doesn't like it when I post promiscuous photos—the next day he calls and he's like, "Hi." Meaning he's so annoyed with me, but let's just put that aside and move on because he knows I'm listening to him but I'm not really going to change *for him*. I honestly look at him like an L.A. father figure.

AUGUST GETTY I met August through his assistant at the time. Another Nick. Not the Nick I just told you about, but Nick Carbone. We were at a club called the Abbey, and Nick asked if I wanted to go to an afterparty at his friend's house. It was August's and I met him there, and we started hanging out. We connected instantly. I don't think we started hanging out right away. I really wish I could go back in time and just watch how we met, because neither of us really remembers exactly. But we started hanging out. And we got really, really, really close really, really, really quickly. And then he made me the muse of his fashion line. We both love fashion and playing dress-up. We're both materialistic. But at the same time, we do dumb things together. Like jumping on buses in the middle of bus lots in the middle of the night. And if you were paying attention, you already know about our burping contests. I can burp on command and am really good, so I obvi always win.

NATS GETTY Nats, as you probably know, has become a really important person in my life. She's August's sister. I was friends with August first, before I met Nats. I knew that she was a designer and an artist. We'd met a few times at his fashion shows, and at parties here and there, but I never really said more than two words to her. Other than, like, "Hi, nice to meet you, how are you?" So we really bonded in Paris in 2015 when we all went to August's fashion presentation, and we spent ten days together. The whole thing was very exciting. I'd never been to Paris before, and I'd never met anyone like Nats before. She's an artist and a clothing designer and literally one of the most creative people. She lives her life completely authentically and I found it interesting and inspiring. Not to mention she is the biggest babe I have ever met in my entire life, and I can't believe I am dating (and now am engaged) to the absolute love of my life. She is such a blessing, and I am grateful for her every day. August had basically become like family to me, and not only was it nice to get to know more of his family, it turned out to be something I could've never imagined. Her company's called Strike Oil, and it's super-swaggy street-style clothing, kind of like everyday unisex stuff.

 **HILARY MONTEZ** She's another person I met through Nick Carbone, and another person I met at the Abbey. Something I was lacking when I moved to L.A. was girlfriends. I was so used to having my core girlfriends in Toronto. It was mostly work and gay guys in L.A. But Hilary and I just hit it off. She's a Libra and she always jokes that she is like a balancing scale for people. It's true, though; her energy is extremely calm and she's so pleasant to be around. We have been doing a lot of traveling recently. We just spent ten days in Australia and we didn't get into a fight at all. She is the actual yin to my yang. She's completely opposite to me; she's just very real. And she was really good at helping me through the hard times with my ex-boyfriend when we broke up. A lot of the times it would be just Hilary and me in my apartment and I would be feeling all my feelings and letting them out like word vomit. She would just say, "Think about what you're doing." She doesn't bullshit, she doesn't see people for their name or their money. If there's a problem, she genuinely wants to help. She embodies being authentic, which is so positive to be around. She's a dope makeup artist and also does my makeup for events, because I don't always want to do it and she's way better at it than I am. I thought I had my face beat down before she did it. Also, sometimes I just want to sit there and have someone pamper me while I Instagram, you know? She'll tell you it's no easy task, though. She's always screaming at me to stop moving because I am so impatient. Sorry, Hil!

MARKUS MOLINARI   Definitely one of my first friends in L.A. I remember the first night we ever met. Huxch (see page 217) introduced me to him. The lights came on at two a.m., and Nick, Markus, and his boyfriend and I went back to Markus's house to have drinks and play with his dog. He showed me these pictures on the wall, oil paintings of Rihanna and Katy Perry. There are pictures of me from that night doing a handstand on his rug in a leotard, living my goddamn life. I instantly loved how funny, spontaneous, and authentic he was. He almost gave off this childlike spirit, and all you wanted to do was laugh. His laughter, mind you, was one of the most infectious things I had ever encountered. I admire his hustle when it comes to work; he literally has so much going on and never stops. It's inspiring. And he's also always been there to say congratulations to me and to be like, "Wow, you've come so far, I'm so proud of you." Zero competition, just love. Real recognizes real, I guess.

TIFFANY "TIFF" NAMTU   Tiffany is my sister—well, not by blood, but you know what I mean! We first met when I would visit my brother Adam at college. Tiffany was his unassuming girlfriend who took me under her wing right away. She let me be who I was (or who I was becoming!). Now she lives in Los Angeles with me! Her relationship with Adam lasted a long time, but ultimately, they did not work out. However, she will always be an important part of my family.

ARI GETTY   Nats's and August's mom. She's kind of been a second mom to me. About a year after Nats and I started dating, Nats told me that Ari said she hopes, one day, she'll see me as her mom since mine is gone now. She hopes I'll call her Mom. I cried after hearing that because it was so beautiful. I don't call her Mom, though. I call her "Mama G" or "Mama Getty." Both her kids are gay and she's really involved with the LGBTQ+ community. Nats was a tomboy and August liked mermaids and heels growing up. She always wanted a little princess, and I'm like the little princess she never had. I love it.

♦
ACKNOWLEDGMENTS

This book would not be possible without the love and support of my YouTube viewers. From day one you've understood me, accepted me, and encouraged me to grow to be exactly who I was always meant to be. You've given me the blessing of sharing my story on a higher level that I never thought I'd get the chance to. From makeup tutorials and beauty product hauls sitting on my bedroom floor in Canada as a teenager to sitting in my Los Angeles home, writing this book, you've been there by my side. And I wanted to say a huge thank you and tell you I love you so much. And of course, stay gorgeous, duh!

A special thank you to Marshall Heyman for your patience, laughter, and support. This book is a result of your hard work. And to my editor, Donna Loffredo, you're the female boss I needed to keep me in check. To Steve Troha who saw the potential and helped sell it right away. Thank you for everything.

My managers, Scott Fisher and Adam Wescott, have never stopped hustling for me and I'm so grateful for them. This book wouldn't be happening without them, that's for sure! Thank you for always pushing me to be greater, bigger, and more authentic than the year before. Our journey is one for the books—literally! God I make myself laugh sometimes. And to Lord Lori for being a fierce new member of the team.

I am indebted to my late mother, Judy Lazzarato, who was the most positive, loving, beautiful woman I've ever known. She taught me what it is to be a woman and to always live with integrity. I want to thank her for the countless life lessons she instilled in my upbringing, and the ones that she continues to teach me to this very day. I hope I make her proud. I love you endlessly, Mom.

Thank you, Dad, for everything you've done for me. Your unconditional love and knowledge has helped me conquer every struggle that has been thrown my way. I know I can always count on you to listen, care, and talk through any situation. Without you, this book wouldn't have been able to happen because, well, I wouldn't be me without you! I got really lucky with the family I was born into, and I am fully aware that you and my brothers are such a blessing. Thank you to them as well, Adam and Cory, you're the best brothers a girl could ask for. I love you so much!

I like to think that when you're a real person, sooner rather than later you'll find yourself surrounded with other real people. I've been so lucky to find life-long friends that I've known since elementary school in Canada and new friends as well in Los Angeles. Both of which I look at like my own family. Through all the good, the bad, and the ugly you've stuck by me. Thank you to them for the unconditional love and friendship we share. I wouldn't be the woman I am today, or have accomplished what I have without you guys. Thank you for pushing me to keep going when I'm down and cheering me on when I need to hear some positivity! This book is for all of you!

And last but definitely not least to my partner in crime and soulmate: my beautiful fiancée Nats. I love you to the moon and back. I'm so excited to spend the rest of my life with you. Here's to the next chapter.

◆

GIGI GORGEOUS

is a YouTube star, transgender activist, television personality, actress, model, and LGBTQ icon with nearly 8 million followers across her social platforms. In 2017, her feature-length documentary, *This Is Everything: Gigi Gorgeous,* premiered at the Sundance Film Festival. She was named one of *Time* magazine's 25 Most Influential People on the Internet and one of *Forbes*'s 30 Under 30. Some of her other awards include YouTuber of the Year at the Shorty Awards and the LogoTV Trailblazing Social Creator Award for her advocacy on behalf of LGBTQ youth. Gigi works closely with several LGBTQ organizations, including GLAAD, the Los Angeles LGBT Center, and the Children's Hospital Los Angeles Center for Transyouth Health and Development.